HAMLYN
ALL COLOUR
QUICK & EASY

FAST SIMPLE DELICIOUS

HAMLYN
ALL COLOUR
QUICK & EASY

over 250 mouthwatering recipes

hamlyn

- Both metric and imperial measurements are given for the recipes. Use one set of measures only, not a mixture of both.

- Ovens should be preheated to the specified temperature. If using a fan-assisted oven, follow the manufacturer's instructions for adjusting the time and temperature. Grills should also be preheated.

- This book includes dishes made with nuts and nut derivatives. It is advisable for those with known allergic reactions to nuts and nut derivatives and those who may be potentially vulnerable to these allergies, such as pregnant and nursing mothers, invalids, the elderly, babies and children, to avoid dishes made with nuts and nut oils. It is also prudent to check the labels of preprepared ingredients for the possible inclusion of nut derivatives.

- The Department of Health advises that eggs should not be consumed raw. This book contains some dishes made with raw or lightly cooked eggs. It is prudent for more vulnerable people, such as pregnant and nursing mothers, invalids, the elderly, babies and young children, to avoid uncooked or lightly cooked dishes made with eggs.

- Meat and poultry should be cooked thoroughly. To test if poultry is cooked, pierce the flesh through the thickest part with a skewer or fork – the juices should run clear, never pink or red.

- Where pepper is listed in the recipe ingredients, always use freshly ground black pepper.

First published in Great Britain in 2007 by Hamlyn,
a division of Octopus Publishing Group Ltd
2–4 Heron Quays, London E14 4JP

Copyright © Octopus Publishing Group Ltd 2007

ISBN-13: 978-0-600-61588-0

ISBN-10: 0-600-61588-X

A CIP catalogue record for this book is available from the British Library

Printed and bound in China

10 9 8 7 6 5 4 3 2 1

Contents

Introduction

We all appreciate and enjoy home-cooked meals, and we are also all aware of how important eating good, wholesome food rather than junk fast food is to our physical, and mental, well-being. But finding enough time and energy in our pressured lives to cook a proper meal is a constant challenge. Help is here at hand with this bumper collection of more than 250 quick and easy recipes, each taking a maximum of just 30 minutes, and some considerably less, to prepare and cook. Choose from speedy yet satisfying soups, snacks and starters; vegetable dishes and salads, made in moments and mouthwatering; pasta, pizza, noodle and rice dishes, both quick and comforting; effortless yet delicious fish and seafood, poultry and game, meat and vegetarian mains; and desserts that are as sumptuous as they are simple.

After-work solutions

At the end of a long, hard day, what we crave and deserve is to fast-forward to an enticing, tasty and nutritious meal, and there are lots of ideas on offer here that will deliver just that. In less time than it takes to heat up a supermarket ready meal, you can rustle up Maple and Mustard Glazed Salmon (see recipe 159), quickly cooked under the grill while you steam some vegetables, or Marinated Tofu with Pak Choi (see recipe 140), simply and speedily stir-fried. If you are in need of something really hearty, Venison Sausages with Spicy Bean Sauce (see recipe 190) or Chorizo and Chickpea Stew (see recipe 210), both using convenient canned pulses, are sure to hit the spot. And for dessert there are some ultra-quick no-cook options, such as Raspberry and Shortcake Mess (see recipe 228) or Pink Grapefruit Parfait (see recipe 227).

Easy entertaining

It's not just everyday meals that can be quick and easy. In under 15 minutes you can serve up a stylish dinner party dish of Angel Hair Pasta with Prawns (see recipe 99), or really impress your guests with the alluringly crispy Duck with Honey and Lime Sauce (see recipe 183) or Grilled Snapper with Salmoriglio (see recipe 155) with its classy Italian garlic, lemon and fresh herb sauce. To round off your dinner on a high note, invite your guests to dip into the luxurious Strawberries with Chocolate Spread (see recipe 260) or wow them with a platter of pastries in the form of Orange Palmiers with Plums (see recipe 235).

Storecupboard staples

The key to producing successful home-cooked dishes with the minimum of fuss is to build up and maintain a storecupboard of good-quality ingredients that can form the basis of a wide variety of meals, with the addition of a few fresh ingredients, or provide that all-important flavouring for fresh ingredients on any given day. These are the most useful items to keep in store:

• **Dried goods** – strand, ribbon and shaped pasta; rice and egg noodles; basmati, quick-cooking white long-grain rice and risotto rice; quick-cooking polenta, cornflour and plain and self-raising flour; couscous and bulgar wheat; ground and whole almonds, walnut halves, cashew nuts and pine nuts; sesame seeds; ready-to-eat dried apricots and figs, sultanas and raisins; brown, caster and icing sugar

• **Canned and bottled foods** – canned pulses, including chickpeas, lentils and beans; canned tomatoes, anchovy fillets, tuna, crabmeat, coconut milk and black cherries; bottled roasted red peppers and artichoke hearts; olives and capers; passata (sieved tomatoes), sun-blush tomatoes, tomato purée and sun-dried tomato paste

• **Flavourings** – dried herbs and spices; wholegrain, Dijon and dry English mustard; red and white wine, balsamic vinegar and rice vinegar; Thai and Indian curry pastes; Worcestershire, Tabasco, soy, Thai fish and hoisin sauces; rice wine, dry sherry, cider, brandy and liqueurs; honey, maple syrup and jam; stock cubes and/or bouillon powder

• **Oils** – sunflower, olive, groundnut and sesame oils

Freezer standbys

A well-stocked freezer can be used to great effect in helping you to cook quick and easy meals. The following are the essentials:

• **Frozen vegetables** – peas, sweetcorn, leaf spinach, broad beans

• **Cooked peeled prawns**

• **Bread** – partly baked baguettes; ciabatta; ready-made pizza dough bases and/or Italian flatbreads; soft flour tortillas; pitta breads

• **Pastry** – filo pastry; ready-rolled puff pastry

• **Berries** – mixed berry fruits and/or raspberries and blueberries

• **Vanilla ice cream**

Time-saving tips

• Cut down on preparation time by opting for pre-prepared ingredients, such as pitted olives, ready-washed mixed salads, fish fillets and ready trimmed and cubed meat.

• Invest in a food processor, which can be used to speed up a variety of tasks, such as chopping ingredients, blending soups and sauces, whipping up batter and making breadcrumbs.

• A heavy-based griddle pan will prove a worthwhile addition to your kitchen, enabling you quickly to cook meat, poultry and game cuts, as well as seafood and vegetables, and all with a delicious chargrilled flavour and appearance.

• Use ready-made sauces and flavourings to add an instant boost to all manner of dishes, such as miso paste for enhancing oriental soups and marinades, pesto and tapenade for pepping up poultry or fish, black bean sauce for jazzing up stir-fries, and cranberry, mint and horseradish sauces as well as redcurrant jelly for giving a lift to meat dishes.

• For preparing desserts in a hurry have some meringue nests and sweet biscuits like amaretti and shortcake fingers in store to crumble up and swirl with cream and fruit, as well as plain dark chocolate for melting.

1 Soups

1 Tomato and almond soup

Preparation time: **5 minutes**	**1 kg (2 lb) vine-ripened tomatoes, roughly chopped**
	2 garlic cloves, crushed
Cooking time: **20 minutes**	**300 ml (½ pint) vegetable stock**
	2 tablespoons extra virgin olive oil
	1 teaspoon caster sugar
Serves: **4**	**100 g (3½ oz) ground almonds, toasted**
	salt and pepper

BASIL OIL
150 ml (¼ pint) extra virgin olive oil
15 g (½ oz) basil leaves

Put the tomatoes in a saucepan with the garlic, stock, oil, sugar and salt and pepper to taste. Bring to the boil, then reduce the heat and simmer gently for 15 minutes.

Meanwhile, to make the basil oil, put the oil, basil leaves and a pinch of salt in a blender or food processor and blend until really smooth. Set aside.

Stir the almonds into the soup, heat through and then serve in warmed bowls, drizzled with the basil oil.

2 Beetroot gazpacho

Preparation time: **15 minutes**	**500 g (1 lb) cooked beetroot in natural juices, drained and chopped**
	1 small onion, roughly chopped
Cooking time: **No cooking**	**2 garlic cloves, roughly chopped**
	2 tomatoes, roughly chopped
	2 tablespoons capers, drained and rinsed
Serves: **4**	**4 baby cornichons, drained, rinsed and chopped**
	25 g (1 oz) dried white breadcrumbs
	600 ml (1 pint) vegetable stock
	150 ml (¼ pint) extra virgin olive oil
	2 tablespoons white wine vinegar
	salt and pepper

TO SERVE
crème fraîche
dill sprigs

Put the beetroot, onion, garlic, tomatoes, capers and cornichons in a food processor and process until smooth. Add the breadcrumbs and pulse. With the machine running, gradually add the stock, oil and vinegar until completely incorporated and smooth. Season to taste with salt and pepper.

Serve in bowls, topped with a spoonful of crème fraîche and some dill sprigs and sprinkled with pepper.

COOK'S NOTES This makes a perfect no-fuss appetizer for entertaining because you can prepare it in advance, leave it in the refrigerator to chill and simply garnish it and serve when you and your guests are ready to eat.

3 Potato soup with parsley

Preparation time:
10 minutes

Cooking time:
20 minutes

Serves: **4**

1.5 litres (2½ pints) beef stock
4 potatoes, peeled and coarsely grated
1 egg yolk
1 hard-boiled egg yolk, mashed
50 ml (2 fl oz) single cream
**50 g (2 oz) Parmesan cheese, freshly
   grated**
1 tablespoon finely chopped parsley
salt and pepper
125 g (4 oz) croûtons, to serve

Pour the stock into a saucepan and bring to the boil. Sprinkle the potatoes with salt and pepper to taste, then drop them into the boiling stock. Cook for about 15 minutes, stirring occasionally.

Meanwhile, beat the egg yolk in a soup tureen and add the mashed hard-boiled egg yolk. Blend the cream, Parmesan and parsley into the egg mixture and whisk together.

Carefully pour 250 ml (8 fl oz) of the stock into the egg mixture. Reheat the remaining stock and potatoes and gradually add to the soup tureen. Sprinkle with croûtons and serve in warmed bowls.

COOK'S NOTES To make croûtons, remove the crusts from 2 slices of white bread, then cut the bread into 1 cm (½ inch) dice. Heat about 2 tablespoons vegetable oil in a heavy-based frying pan, add the bread cubes and cook, turning and stirring frequently, for 5 minutes or until golden and crisp all over. Remove with a slotted spoon and drain on kitchen paper.

4 Minestrone

Preparation time:
5 minutes

Cooking time:
25 minutes

Serves: **4**

2 tablespoons olive oil
1 onion, chopped
1 garlic clove, crushed
2 celery sticks, chopped
1 leek, finely sliced
1 carrot, chopped
400 g (13 oz) can chopped tomatoes
**600 ml (1 pint) chicken stock or vegetable
   stock**
1 courgette, diced
½ small cabbage, shredded
1 bay leaf
75 g (3 oz) canned haricot beans, drained
**75 g (3 oz) dried spaghetti, broken into
   small pieces, or small pasta shapes**
1 tablespoon chopped flat leaf parsley
salt and pepper
**50 g (2 oz) Parmesan cheese, freshly
   grated, to serve**

Heat the oil in a large saucepan. Add the onion, garlic, celery, leek and carrot and cook over a medium heat, stirring occasionally, for about 3 minutes.

Add the tomatoes, stock, courgette, cabbage, bay leaf and haricot beans. Bring to the boil, lower the heat and simmer for 10 minutes.

Add the pasta and season to taste with salt and pepper. Stir well and cook for a further 8 minutes. Keep stirring because the soup may stick to the base of the pan. Just before serving, add the parsley and stir well. Ladle the soup into warmed bowls and serve with grated Parmesan.

5 Pea, lettuce and lemon soup

Preparation time:
10 minutes

Cooking time:
20 minutes

Serves: **4**

Oven temperature:
200°C (400°F) Gas Mark 6

25 g (1 oz) butter
1 large onion, finely chopped
425 g (14 oz) frozen peas
2 Little Gem lettuces, roughly chopped
1 litre (1¾ pints) vegetable or chicken stock
finely grated rind and juice of ½ lemon
salt and pepper

SESAME CROÛTONS
2 thick slices of bread, crusts removed, cubed
1 tablespoon olive oil
1 tablespoon sesame seeds

To make the sesame croûtons, brush the bread cubes with the oil and put in a roasting tin. Sprinkle with the sesame seeds and bake in a preheated oven, 200°C (400°F), Gas Mark 6, for 10–15 minutes until golden.

Meanwhile, heat the butter in a large saucepan, add the onion and cook for 5 minutes until softened. Add the peas, lettuce, stock, lemon rind and juice and salt and pepper to taste. Bring to the boil, then reduce the heat, cover and simmer for 10–15 minutes.

Leave the soup to cool slightly, then transfer to a blender or food processor and blend until smooth. Return the soup to the pan, adjust the seasoning, if necessary, and heat through. Spoon into warmed bowls and sprinkle with the sesame croûtons.

COOK'S NOTES To save time, you can prepare the croûtons in advance. Simply store them in an airtight container until you make the soup later on.

6 Chilli bean soup

Preparation time:
5 minutes

Cooking time:
25 minutes

Serves: **3–4**

2 tablespoons olive oil
1 onion, chopped
1 garlic clove, crushed
1 teaspoon hot chilli powder
1 teaspoon ground coriander
½ teaspoon ground cumin
400 g (13 oz) can red kidney beans, drained and rinsed
400 g (13 oz) can chopped tomatoes
600 ml (1 pint) vegetable stock
12 tortilla chips
50 g (2 oz) Cheddar cheese, grated
salt and pepper
soured cream, to serve

Heat the oil in a saucepan, add the onion, garlic, chilli powder, coriander and cumin and cook, stirring frequently, for 5 minutes or until the onion has softened. Add the beans, tomatoes, stock and salt and pepper to taste.

Bring the soup to the boil, then reduce the heat, cover and simmer for 15 minutes. Transfer to a blender or food processor and blend until fairly smooth. Return the soup to the pan and heat through.

Pour the soup into heatproof bowls. Top with the tortilla chips, scatter over the Cheddar and put under a preheated high grill for 1–2 minutes until the cheese has melted. Serve immediately with soured cream.

7 Summer vegetable soup

8 Garlic and paprika soup with egg

Preparation time:
10 minutes

Cooking time:
20 minutes

Serves: **4**

1 teaspoon olive oil
1 leek, thinly sliced
1 large potato, peeled and chopped
450 g (14½ oz) prepared mixed summer
vegetables, such as peas, asparagus
spears, broad beans and courgettes
2 tablespoons chopped mint
900 ml (1½ pints) vegetable stock
2 tablespoons crème fraîche
salt (optional) and pepper

Preparation time:
10 minutes

Cooking time:
20 minutes

Serves: **4**

4 tablespoons olive oil
12 thick slices of baguette
5 garlic cloves, sliced
1 onion, finely chopped
1 tablespoon paprika
1 teaspoon ground cumin
good pinch of saffron threads
1.2 litres (2 pints) vegetable stock
25 g (1 oz) dried soup pasta
4 eggs
salt and pepper

Heat the oil in a medium saucepan, add the leek and potato and cook for 3–4 minutes until softened.

Add the mixed vegetables to the pan with the mint and the stock and bring to the boil. Reduce the heat and simmer for 10 minutes.

Transfer the soup to a blender or food processor and blend until smooth. Return the soup to the pan with the crème fraîche and season to taste with salt, if you like, and pepper. Heat through and serve in warmed bowls.

Heat the oil in a heavy-based saucepan, add the bread and cook gently, turning once, until golden. Remove with a slotted spoon and drain on kitchen paper.

Add the garlic, onion, paprika and cumin to the pan and cook gently, stirring, for 3 minutes. Add the saffron threads and stock and bring to the boil. Stir in the pasta. Reduce the heat, cover and simmer for 8 minutes or until the pasta is tender but still firm to the bite. Season to taste with salt and pepper.

Break the eggs on to a saucer and slide them into the pan one at a time. Cook for 2 minutes or until just set.

Stack 3 fried bread slices in each of 4 warmed bowls. Ladle the soup over the bread, making sure that each serving contains an egg. Serve immediately.

COOK'S NOTES Frozen vegetables make a quick and easy alternative to fresh, as they are prepared and ready to cook. Freshly frozen vegetables retain all their nutrients and goodness.

9 Cauliflower and cumin soup

10 Spinach and broccoli soup

Preparation time: **10 minutes**	**1 teaspoon vegetable oil** **1 onion, chopped** **1 garlic clove, crushed**
Cooking time: **20 minutes**	**1 teaspoon cumin seeds** **1 cauliflower, cut into florets** **1 large potato, peeled and chopped**
Serves: **4**	**450 ml (¾ pint) vegetable stock** **450 ml (¾ pint) milk** **2 tablespoons crème fraîche** **2 tablespoons chopped fresh coriander** **salt (optional) and pepper**

Heat the oil in a medium saucepan, add the onion, garlic and cumin seeds and cook, stirring, for 3–4 minutes until the onion is softened. Add the cauliflower, potato, stock and milk and bring to the boil. Reduce the heat and simmer for 15 minutes.

Transfer the soup to a blender or food processor and blend until smooth. Return it to the pan with the crème fraîche and coriander and season to taste with salt, if you like, and pepper. Heat through and serve in warmed bowls.

Preparation time: **10 minutes**	**2 tablespoons olive oil** **50 g (2 oz) butter** **1 onion, diced**
Cooking time: **20 minutes**	**1 garlic clove, finely chopped** **2 potatoes, peeled and diced** **250 g (8 oz) broccoli, chopped**
Serves: **4**	**300 g (10 oz) spinach, chopped** **900 ml (1½ pints) vegetable or chicken** **stock** **125 g (4 oz) Gorgonzola cheese, crumbled** **2 tablespoons lemon juice** **½ teaspoon freshly grated nutmeg** **salt and pepper** **75 g (3 oz) toasted pine nuts, to garnish** **warm crusty bread, to serve**

Heat the oil and butter in a saucepan, add the onion and garlic and cook for 3 minutes. Add the potatoes, broccoli, spinach and stock and bring to the boil, then reduce the heat and simmer for 15 minutes.

If you like, transfer the soup to a blender or food processor and blend until smooth. Return it to the pan and heat through. Add the Gorgonzola with the lemon juice, nutmeg and salt and pepper to taste and stir well. Spoon into warmed soup bowls, garnish with toasted pine nuts and serve with warm crusty bread.

COOK'S NOTES This soup is especially delicious served with multigrain bread topped with melted Gruyère cheese.

11 Butter bean soup

Preparation time:
5 minutes

Cooking time:
20 minutes

Serves: **4**

3 tablespoons olive oil
1 onion, finely chopped
2 celery sticks, thinly sliced
2 garlic cloves, thinly sliced
2 x 400 g (13 oz) cans butter beans,
drained and rinsed
4 tablespoons sun-dried tomato paste
900 ml (1½ pints) vegetable stock
1 tablespoon chopped rosemary or thyme
salt and pepper
fresh Parmesan cheese shavings, to
serve

Heat the oil in a saucepan, add the onion and cook for 3 minutes. Add the celery and garlic and cook for 2 minutes.

Add the beans, sun-dried tomato paste, stock, rosemary or thyme and a little salt and pepper. Bring to the boil, then reduce the heat, cover and simmer gently for 15 minutes. Serve the soup in warmed bowls, sprinkled with Parmesan shavings.

12 Tuscan bean soup

Preparation time:
10 minutes

Cooking time:
20 minutes

Serves: **4**

2 tablespoons olive oil
4 shallots, chopped
2 garlic cloves, crushed
150 g (5 oz) piece of green bacon, diced
1 carrot, diced
2 celery sticks, diced
½ red pepper, cored, deseeded and diced
400 g (13 oz) can borlotti beans, drained
and rinsed
1 litre (1¾ pints) chicken stock
1 bay leaf
1 teaspoon chopped oregano
1 teaspoon chopped marjoram
handful of flat leaf parsley, chopped
salt and pepper
extra virgin olive oil, for drizzling

Heat the olive oil in a saucepan, add the shallots, garlic, bacon, carrot, celery and red pepper and cook for 5 minutes.

Add the beans, stock, bay leaf, oregano and marjoram and bring to the boil. Reduce the heat and simmer for 15 minutes. Skim off any scum that rises to the surface from the beans. Taste and season well.

Just before serving, add the chopped parsley. Ladle the soup into warmed bowls and drizzle each one with a little extra virgin olive oil.

COOK'S NOTES This nutritious soup is perfect for speedy lunches or dinners. Serve with crusty bread for a more substantial meal.

13 Gazpacho

Preparation time:
15 minutes, plus chilling

Cooking time:
No cooking

Serves: **6**

2 garlic cloves, roughly chopped
¼ teaspoon salt
3 thick slices of white bread, crusts removed
1 kg (2 lb) tomatoes, skinned and roughly chopped
2 onions, roughly chopped
½ large cucumber, peeled, deseeded and roughly chopped
2 large green peppers, cored, deseeded and roughly chopped
5 tablespoons olive oil
4 tablespoons white wine vinegar
1 litre (1¾ pints) iced water
pepper
small ice cubes, to serve

Combine the garlic and salt in a mortar and pound with a pestle until smooth. Put the bread into a bowl, cover with cold water and leave to soak for 5 seconds. Drain the bread, then squeeze out the moisture.

Set aside a quarter of the tomatoes, onions, cucumber and green peppers for garnishing. Put the remaining vegetables in a food processor. Add the garlic paste, bread and oil and process until smooth.

Pour the mixture into a bowl and stir in the vinegar and measured iced water with pepper to taste. Cover and chill in the freezer for 15 minutes.

Meanwhile, chop the reserved vegetables finely. Serve the soup in chilled bowls, adding 2–3 ice cubes to each bowl and topping the soup with the chopped vegetables.

14 Quick and easy miso soup

Preparation time:
5 minutes

Cooking time:
8 minutes

Serves: **4**

1 litre (1¾ pints) vegetable stock
2 tablespoons miso paste
125 g (4 oz) shiitake mushrooms, sliced
200 g (7 oz) firm tofu, cubed
fresh bread, to serve

Pour the stock into a saucepan and bring to a simmer.

Add the miso paste, mushrooms and tofu to the stock and simmer gently for 5 minutes. Serve in warmed bowls with bread.

COOK'S NOTES Just a few ingredients produce a soup that is packed full of flavour. Serve as a starter to a Japanese meal or on its own for a light lunch.

15 Beef and noodle broth

Preparation time: **15 minutes**	**300 g (10 oz) rump or sirloin steak**
	15 g (½ oz) fresh root ginger, peeled and grated
Cooking time: **10 minutes**	**2 teaspoons soy sauce**
	600 ml (1 pint) beef or chicken stock
	1 red chilli, deseeded and finely chopped
Serves: **2**	**1 garlic clove, thinly sliced**
	2 teaspoons caster sugar
	50 g (2 oz) dried vermicelli rice noodles
	2 teaspoons vegetable oil
	75 g (3 oz) sugar snap peas, halved lengthways
	small handful of Thai basil, torn into pieces

Trim any fat from the steak. Mix the ginger with half the soy sauce and spread over both sides of the steak.

Pour the stock into a saucepan and add the chilli, garlic and sugar. Bring to a gentle simmer and cook for 5 minutes.

Meanwhile, soak the noodles in a saucepan of boiling water according to the packet instructions. Drain and rinse thoroughly under cold running water.

Heat the oil in a small, heavy-based frying pan, add the beef and cook for 2 minutes on each side. Transfer the meat to a board, cut it in half lengthways and then cut it across into thin strips.

Add the noodles, sugar snap peas, basil and remaining soy sauce to the soup and heat gently for 1 minute. Stir in the beef and serve immediately in warmed bowls.

16 Black bean soup with soba

Preparation time: **10 minutes**	**200 g (7 oz) dried soba (Japanese noodles)**
	2 tablespoons groundnut or vegetable oil
Cooking time: **8 minutes**	**1 bunch of spring onions, sliced**
	2 garlic cloves, roughly chopped
	1 red chilli, deseeded and sliced
Serves: **4**	**3.5 cm (1½ inch) piece of fresh root ginger, peeled and grated**
	125 ml (4 fl oz) black bean sauce or black bean stir-fry sauce
	750 ml (1¼ pints) vegetable stock
	200 g (7 oz) pak choi or spring greens, shredded
	2 teaspoons soy sauce
	1 teaspoon caster sugar
	50 g (2 oz) unsalted raw peanuts

Bring a large saucepan of water to the boil, add the noodles and cook for 5 minutes, or according to the packet instructions, until just tender.

Meanwhile, heat the oil in a saucepan, add the spring onions and garlic and cook gently for 1 minute.

Add the chilli, ginger, black bean sauce and stock and bring to the boil. Stir in the pak choi or spring greens, soy sauce, sugar and peanuts, then reduce the heat and simmer gently for 4 minutes.

Drain the noodles, rinse with fresh hot water and spoon into the base of 4 warmed bowls. Ladle the soup over the top and serve immediately.

17 Thai prawn broth

Preparation time:
15 minutes

Cooking time:
10 minutes

Serves: **4**

1.2 litres (2 pints) vegetable stock
2 teaspoons red Thai curry paste
4 kaffir lime leaves, torn into pieces
4 teaspoons Thai fish sauce
2 spring onions, sliced
150 g (5 oz) shiitake mushrooms, sliced
125 g (4 oz) dried soba (Japanese noodles)
½ red pepper, cored, deseeded and diced
125 g (4 oz) pak choi, thinly sliced
250 g (8 oz) frozen prawns, defrosted and rinsed
small bunch of fresh coriander leaves, torn into pieces

Pour the stock into a saucepan and add the curry paste, lime leaves, fish sauce, onions and mushrooms. Bring to the boil, then reduce the heat and simmer for 5 minutes.

Meanwhile, bring a separate saucepan of water to the boil, add the noodles and cook for 5 minutes, or according to the packet instructions, until just tender.

Add the remaining ingredients to the soup and cook for 2 minutes until piping hot.

Drain the noodles, rinse with fresh hot water and spoon into the base of 4 warmed bowls. Ladle the hot prawn broth over the top and serve immediately.

COOK'S NOTES If you are serving this soup to vegetarians, leave out the prawns and fish sauce.

18 Fragrant tofu and noodle soup

Preparation time:
10 minutes

Cooking time:
10 minutes

Serves: **2**

125 g (4 oz) firm tofu, diced
1 tablespoon sesame oil
75 g (3 oz) dried thin rice noodles
600 ml (1 pint) vegetable stock
2.5 cm (1 inch) piece of fresh root ginger, peeled and thickly sliced
1 large garlic clove, thickly sliced
3 kaffir lime leaves, torn into pieces
2 lemon grass stalks, halved
handful of spinach or pak choi
50 g (2 oz) bean sprouts
1–2 red chillies, to taste, deseeded and thinly sliced
2 tablespoons chopped fresh coriander
1 tablespoon Thai fish sauce

TO SERVE
lime wedges
chilli sauce

Put the tofu on a plate covered with kitchen paper and leave to stand for 5 minutes to drain.

Heat the oil in a wok or large frying pan, add the tofu and stir-fry for 2–3 minutes or until golden brown all over. Remove with a slotted spoon and drain on kitchen paper.

Meanwhile, soak the noodles in a saucepan of boiling water according to the packet instructions. Drain, rinse thoroughly under cold running water and drain again.

Put the stock in a large saucepan, add the ginger, garlic, lime leaves and lemon grass and bring to the boil. Reduce the heat, add the tofu, noodles, spinach or pak choi, bean sprouts and chillies and heat through for 2 minutes. Stir in the coriander and fish sauce, then pour into warmed deep bowls to serve. Serve with lime wedges and chilli sauce.

19 Prawn and noodle soup # 20 Hot and sour soup

Preparation time:
5 minutes

Cooking time:
15 minutes

Serves: **4**

**900 ml (1½ pints) vegetable or chicken
 stock
2 kaffir lime leaves, torn into pieces
1 lemon grass stalk, lightly bruised
150 g (5 oz) dried egg noodles
50 g (2 oz) frozen peas
50 g (2 oz) frozen sweetcorn
100 g (3½ oz) large cooked peeled prawns
4 spring onions, sliced
2 teaspoons soy sauce**

Pour the stock into a large saucepan and add the lime leaves and
lemon grass. Bring to the boil, then reduce the heat and simmer for
10 minutes.

Add the noodles to the pan and cook according to the packet
instructions, adding the remaining ingredients after 2 minutes of
cooking. Serve in warmed bowls.

Preparation time:
10 minutes

Cooking time:
10 minutes

Serves: **4**

**1 litre (1¾ pints) fish stock
4 kaffir lime leaves, torn into pieces
4 slices of peeled fresh root ginger
1 red chilli, deseeded and sliced
1 lemon grass stalk
125 g (4 oz) mushrooms, sliced
100 g (3½ oz) dried rice noodles
75 g (3 oz) baby spinach leaves
125 g (4 oz) cooked peeled tiger prawns
2 tablespoons lemon juice
pepper**

Pour the stock into a large saucepan and add the lime leaves, ginger,
chilli and lemon grass. Cover and bring to the boil. Add the mushrooms,
reduce the heat and simmer for 2 minutes.

Break the noodles into short lengths, drop them into the soup and
simmer for 3 minutes.

Add the spinach and prawns and simmer for 2 minutes until the prawns
are heated through. Add the lemon juice. Remove and discard the lemon
grass stalk and season the soup with pepper then serve in warmed bowls.

COOK'S NOTES The addition of kaffir lime leaves and lemon grass
results in a fresh, zingy soup that is a meal in a bowl.

2 Snacks and Starters

21 Fennel and anchovy crostini

22 Tomato bruschetta

Preparation time:
10 minutes

Cooking time:
8–10 minutes

Serves: **4**

Oven temperature:
220°C (425°F) Gas Mark 7

12 slices of baguette
1 fennel bulb, trimmed
1 small garlic clove, crushed
2 tablespoons chopped parsley
6 tablespoons extra virgin olive oil
2 tablespoons lemon juice
24 bottled marinated anchovy fillets, drained
salt and pepper

Arrange the bread slices on a baking sheet and cook in a preheated oven, 220°C (425°F), Gas Mark 7, for 8–10 minutes until crisp and golden, turning halfway through. Transfer to a serving platter.

Remove the tough outer layer of fennel and discard. Cut the bulb in half lengthways and then cut it crossways into wafer-thin slices (you will need about 100 g (3½ oz) of prepared fennel). Put in a bowl with the garlic and parsley. Add the oil, lemon juice and salt and pepper to taste and toss together until well coated.

Spoon the fennel mixture on to the crostini and top each with 2 anchovy fillets. Drizzle over any remaining dressing from the bowl.

Preparation time:
10 minutes

Cooking time:
5 minutes

Serves: **1**

12 cherry tomatoes
50 g (2 oz) mozzarella cheese
3 thick slices of ciabatta
olive oil, for brushing
a few basil leaves

Chop the tomatoes into small pieces and thinly slice the mozzarella.

Lightly toast the ciabatta on both sides under a preheated high grill. Brush with a little oil, then arrange the mozzarella and tomatoes on the toast. Tear the basil leaves into small pieces and scatter them over the bruschetta.

Cook the bruschetta under the grill until the cheese has melted slightly. Serve immediately.

COOK'S NOTES These bruschetta are an ideal starter as you can prepare the mozzarella and tomatoes in advance and the whole dish is ready in a matter of minutes.

23 Mediterranean bruschetta

Preparation time:
10 minutes

Cooking time:
10 minutes

Serves: **4**

1 yellow pepper, cored, deseeded and cut lengthways into 8 strips
1 red pepper, cored, deseeded and cut lengthways into 8 strips
2 courgettes, diagonally sliced
1 red onion, sliced and separated into rings
4 tablespoons olive oil
2 garlic cloves, peeled but left whole
1 ciabatta loaf or baguette
1 small tomato, halved
salt and pepper
8–12 basil leaves, to garnish

Arrange the peppers, courgettes and onion in a single layer on a grill rack. Brush with a little of the oil and rub with the garlic. Put under a preheated grill on its highest setting and cook the vegetables on one side only for 5 minutes or until lightly browned but still firm. Set aside and keep warm.

Cut the bread diagonally into medium-thick slices and toast on both sides under the grill. Rub the top of each slice with the garlic and tomato, then pile the grilled vegetables on top.

Drizzle the remaining oil over the vegetables and season well with salt and pepper. Garnish with basil leaves and serve immediately.

24 Butterbean, anchovy and coriander pâté

Preparation time:
10 minutes

Cooing time:
No cooking

Serves: **2–3**

400 g (13 oz) can butter beans, drained and rinsed
50 g (2 oz) drained anchovy fillets in oil
2 spring onions, finely chopped
2 tablespoons lemon juice
1 tablespoon olive oil
4 tablespoons chopped fresh coriander
salt and pepper

TO SERVE
lemon wedges
toasted rye bread

Put all the ingredients, except the coriander, in a blender or food processor and blend until well mixed but not smooth. Alternatively, mash the beans with a fork, finely chop the anchovies and mix the ingredients together by hand.

Stir in the coriander and season well with salt and pepper. Transfer to a serving dish. Serve with lemon wedges and toasted rye bread.

COOK'S NOTES You can use other canned beans in place of the butter beans, such as cannellini or red kidney beans.

25 Warm turkey focaccia

26 Oven-roasted mushrooms on toast

Preparation time: **10 minutes**	**1 tablespoon olive oil** **250 g (8 oz) boneless, skinless turkey** **breast, cut into thin strips**
Cooking time: **10 minutes**	**1 onion, thinly sliced** **2 focaccia loaves, thickly sliced** **2 tablespoons black olive tapenade**
Serves: **4**	**100 g (3½ oz) sun-dried tomatoes in oil,** **drained (oil reserved) and sliced** **4 tomatoes, roughly chopped** **handful of basil leaves (optional)** **salt and pepper** **rocket leaves, to serve**

Heat the oil in a large frying pan, add the turkey and onion and cook for 5 minutes until the turkey is lightly browned all over and cooked through.

Meanwhile, lightly toast the focaccia slices on both sides. Spread thinly with the olive tapenade and drizzle with a little of the reserved oil from the sun-dried tomatoes.

Add the fresh and sun-dried tomatoes to the turkey with the basil, if using, and season to taste with salt and pepper. Cook for 3 minutes or until heated through, then spoon on to the toasted focaccia and top with rocket leaves. Serve immediately.

Preparation time: **10 minutes**	**8 large flat mushrooms, trimmed** **2 garlic cloves, crushed** **125 ml (4 fl oz) extra virgin olive oil**
Cooking time: **20 minutes**	**2 teaspoons chopped thyme** **finely grated rind and juice of 1 lemon** **2 tablespoons chopped parsley**
Serves: **4**	**salt and pepper**
Oven temperature: **220°C (425°F) Gas Mark 7**	TO SERVE **4 slices of buttered toast** **rocket leaves** **fresh Parmesan cheese shavings**

Put the mushrooms, stalk sides up, in a large roasting tin and season to taste with salt and pepper. Put the garlic, oil and thyme in a small bowl. Add the lemon rind, reserving a little for garnishing, then mix together. Spoon half the oil mixture over the mushrooms.

Roast the mushrooms in a preheated oven, 220°C (425°F), Gas Mark 7, for 20 minutes or until tender. Sprinkle with the parsley and drizzle over the lemon juice.

Arrange the mushrooms on the buttered toast, drizzle over the remaining oil mixture and serve topped with rocket leaves and Parmesan shavings and garnish with the reserved lemon rind.

COOK'S NOTES **The olive tapenade, made from crushed black olives, gives an instant boost to the flavour of these open sandwiches.**

COOK'S NOTES **Use mushrooms that are of an equal size so that they cook evenly.**

27 Smoky hummus with warm flatbread

28 Broad bean, pear and pecorino crostini

Preparation time:
10 minutes

Cooking time:
20 minutes

Serves: 4

Oven temperature:
160°C (325°F) Gas Mark 3

400 g (13 oz) can chickpeas, drained and rinsed
3 tablespoons lemon juice
1 large garlic clove, crushed
2 tablespoons tahini paste
1 teaspoon hot smoked paprika, plus extra for sprinkling
½ teaspoon ground cumin
150 ml (¼ pint) extra virgin olive oil, plus extra for drizzling
2 tablespoons sesame seeds
salt and pepper

TO SERVE
4 sheets of Lebanese or Turkish flatbread
crunchy raw vegetables (optional)

Put all the ingredients, except the oil and sesame seeds, in a blender or food processor and blend until smooth. With the machine running, very slowly drizzle in the oil until it is completely incorporated. Season to taste with salt and pepper and scrape into a serving dish.

Wrap the flatbread in foil and heat in a preheated oven, 160°C (325°F), Gas Mark 3, for 20 minutes until warmed through.

Meanwhile, heat a nonstick frying pan, add the sesame seeds and cook, stirring constantly, for 2–3 minutes until lightly browned. Stir most of the toasted sesame seeds into the hummus and sprinkle the remainder over the top. Drizzle the hummus with oil, sprinkle with paprika and serve with the flatbread and raw vegetables, if you like.

Preparation time:
10 minutes

Cooking time:
15 minutes

Serves: 6

Oven temperature:
190°C (375°F) Gas Mark 5

1 thin French baguette
extra virgin olive oil, for brushing and mixing
250 g (8 oz) fresh broad beans, shelled
1 small ripe pear, peeled, cored and finely chopped
drop of balsamic or sherry vinegar
125 g (4 oz) pecorino, salted ricotta or feta cheese, cut into small cubes
salt and pepper

Slice the bread into thin rounds, brush them with olive oil and arrange on a baking sheet. Bake in a preheated oven, 190°C (375°F), Gas Mark 5, for about 10 minutes or until golden and crisp.

Meanwhile, blanch the beans for 3 minutes in a saucepan of boiling water. Drain and refresh in cold water. Pop the beans out of their skins. Mash them roughly using a fork, moisten with a little olive oil and season well with salt and pepper.

Mix the chopped pear with a drop of balsamic or sherry vinegar. Stir in the cubes of cheese. Spread each crostini with a mound of bean purée and top with a spoonful of the pear and cheese mixture. Serve immediately.

COOK'S NOTES If you can't get hold of Lebanese or Turkish flatbread, pitta breads or even soft flour tortillas would make a good substitute.

29 Haloumi with lemon and paprika

30 Thai fishcakes with sweet chilli sauce

Preparation time:
5 minutes

Cooking time:
5 minutes

Serves: **4**

6 tablespoons extra virgin olive oil
4 tablespoons lemon juice
½ teaspoon smoked paprika
250 g (8 oz) haloumi cheese, cut into chunks
salt and pepper

Mix the oil, lemon juice and paprika together in a small bowl and season to taste with salt and pepper.

Heat a heavy-based frying pan until hot, add the haloumi and toss over a medium heat until golden.

Immediately transfer to a serving plate, drizzle over the oil mixture and serve with cocktail sticks to spike the haloumi chunks.

Preparation time:
15 minutes

Cooking time:
15 minutes

Serves: **4**

250 g (8 oz) raw tiger prawns, peeled and deveined
250 g (8 oz) firm white fish, such as haddock, cod or ling, diced
4 kaffir lime leaves, very finely chopped
4 spring onions, finely chopped
2 tablespoons chopped fresh coriander
1 small egg, beaten
2 tablespoons Thai fish sauce
65 g (2½ oz) rice flour
sunflower oil, for shallow-frying
lime wedges, to garnish
sweet chilli sauce, to serve

Put all the ingredients, except the oil, in a food processor and pulse briefly until blended. Use wet hands to shape the mixture into 12 flat cakes about 5 cm (2 inches) across.

Heat 1 cm (½ inch) oil in a frying pan, add the fishcakes, in batches, and cook for 2 minutes on each side until golden. Remove with a slotted spoon and drain on kitchen paper. Keep the cooked fishcakes warm in a low oven while cooking the remainder.

Garnish with lime wedges and serve with sweet chilli sauce for dipping.

COOK'S NOTES Haloumi is a semi-hard ewes' milk cheese from Cyprus with a wonderfully salty, sharp flavour, which really comes into its own with this quick and easy treatment – the outside becomes deliciously crisp and the inside meltingly soft.

31 Vegetable tempura with dipping sauce

Preparation time:
20 minutes

Cooking time:
about 10 minutes

Serves: **4**

DIPPING SAUCE
2.5 cm (1 inch) piece of fresh root ginger, peeled and grated
½ red chilli, deseeded and finely chopped
4 tablespoons soy sauce
2 tablespoons dry sherry
4 tablespoons vegetable stock
1 garlic clove, finely chopped

VEGETABLES
500 g (1 lb) broccoli florets, sliced
150 g (5 oz) cup mushrooms, thinly sliced
150 g (5 oz) baby sweetcorn
150 g (5 oz) mangetout
75 g (3 oz) baby red Swiss chard leaves

TEMPURA BATTER
1 egg
100 ml (3½ fl oz) iced water
50 g (2 oz) plain flour
40 g (1½ oz) cornflour
½ teaspoon baking powder
¼ teaspoon salt
sunflower oil, for deep-frying

Mix all the dipping sauce ingredients together in a small bowl and divide among 4 small dishes. Arrange the vegetables in individual groups. To make the batter, mix the egg and water together in a bowl. Gradually whisk in the dry ingredients until smooth.

Half-fill a large saucepan with oil and heat to 180–190°C (350–375°F), or until a cube of bread browns in 30 seconds. Drop a small handful of the vegetables into the batter. Lift them out one at a time, draining the excess, add to the oil, in small batches, and cook for 2–3 minutes until crisp. Remove with a slotted spoon and drain on kitchen paper. Keep warm in a low oven while cooking the remainder. Divide the vegetables among serving plates and add the bowls of dipping sauce.

32 Lemon grass fish skewers

Preparation time:
10 minutes

Cooking time:
4–5 minutes

Serves: **4**

500 g (1 lb) skinless haddock fillets, chopped
1 tablespoon chopped mint
2 tablespoons chopped fresh coriander
2 teaspoons red Thai curry paste
2 kaffir lime leaves, finely chopped, or finely grated rind of 1 lime
2 lemon grass stalks, quartered lengthways
olive oil, for brushing

TO SERVE
sweet chilli sauce
lime wedges

Put the fish, mint, coriander, curry paste and lime leaves or rind in a food processor and process for 30 seconds until well combined.

Divide the mixture into 8 portions, then mould each portion around a lemon grass stalk 'skewer', forming it into a sausage shape.

Brush with a little oil, then cook under a preheated high grill, turning occasionally, for 4–5 minutes until cooked through. Serve with a little sweet chilli sauce and lime wedges.

COOK'S NOTES If you have time, soak the lemon grass stalks in cold water for 30 minutes to prevent them from burning under the grill.

33 Thai chicken shells with coconut rice

34 Melon trio with green tea

Preparation time:
10 minutes

Cooking time:
15 minutes

Serves: **4**

1 teaspoon vegetable oil
2 chicken breasts, about 150 g (5 oz)
   each, sliced
1 tablespoon red or green Thai curry
   paste
400 ml (14 fl oz) can coconut milk

RICE
250 g (8 oz) basmati rice
100 ml (3½ fl oz) water
3 tablespoons chopped fresh coriander

TO SERVE
3 spring onions, sliced
4 Little Gem lettuces, separated into
   individual leaves
2 limes, cut into wedges

Heat the oil in a nonstick frying pan, add the chicken and cook for 2 minutes.

Add the curry paste and stir-fry for 1 minute. Add half the coconut milk and bring to the boil, then reduce the heat and simmer gently for 10 minutes.

Meanwhile, put the rice in a saucepan with the remaining coconut milk and measured water. Bring to the boil, then reduce the heat, cover and simmer for 10–12 minutes until all the liquid has been absorbed, adding a little extra water if necessary. Stir through the coriander.

To serve, spoon a little of the chicken mixture, spring onion and rice on to the individual lettuce leaves. Serve with the lime wedges.

Preparation time:
15 minutes, plus
cooling/chilling

Cooking time:
No cooking

Serves: **6**

2 orange-flavoured green teabags
300 ml (½ pint) boiling water
1 orange-fleshed cantaloupe melon, such
   as charentais
½ green-fleshed melon, such as galia or
   ogen
½ honeydew melon
2 tablespoons light cane sugar
finely grated rind and juice of 1 lime

TO GARNISH
lime wedges
6 fresh lychees

Put the teabags in a heatproof jug and pour over the measured boiling water. Leave to infuse for 2 minutes. Lift out the bags, draining well. Break open one of the bags, remove a few tea leaves and add to the tea infusion. Leave to cool for 15 minutes.

Meanwhile, halve the whole melon, scoop out the seeds and discard. Deseed the other melons. Cut away the skin with a small knife. Cut the orange- and green-fleshed melons into long, thin slices and dice the honeydew melon. Put all the melon into a large, shallow dish, cover and chill in the freezer while the tea is cooling.

Sprinkle the sugar and lime rind and juice over the melon and pour over the tea. Arrange the long melon slices in fan shapes on individual serving plates. Spoon the diced melon alongside and serve each one with lime wedges and a partially peeled lychee.

COOK'S NOTES These impressive chicken shells would also be great for buffets or drinks parties, as they can be eaten by hand.

COOK'S NOTES Don't be tempted to leave the tea to infuse for longer than 2 minutes, or it will taste bitter.

35 Figs with ricotta and Parma ham

36 Smoked salmon Thai rolls

Preparation time:
10 minutes

Cooking time:
No cooking

Serves: **4**

8 ripe figs
1 teaspoon Dijon mustard
125 g (4 oz) ricotta cheese
85 g (3¼ oz) Parma ham
2 tablespoons balsamic vinegar
salt and pepper

Preparation time:
15 minutes

Cooking time:
No cooking

Makes: **12**

12 slices of smoked salmon
1 cucumber, peeled, deseeded and cut into matchsticks
1 long red chilli, deseeded and thinly sliced
handful each of fresh coriander, mint and Thai basil leaves

DRESSING
2 tablespoons sweet chilli sauce
2 tablespoons clear honey
2 tablespoons lime juice
1 tablespoon Thai fish sauce

Cut a cross down through each fig, but not completely through the base. Open out slightly.

Stir the mustard into the ricotta in a bowl and season to taste with salt and pepper.

Divide the ricotta mixture among the figs, spooning it over the top. Put 2 figs on each serving plate and top with an equal quantity of the Parma ham. Serve drizzled with the vinegar.

Separate the smoked salmon slices and lay out flat on a work surface. Divide the cucumber, chilli and herbs among the smoked salmon slices, arranging them in a mound on each slice.

Mix all the dressing ingredients together in a small bowl and drizzle over the filling. Roll up the salmon slices to enclose the filling and serve on a large platter.

COOK'S NOTES Thai basil, which has purplish stems, has a slight aniseed flavour.

37 Red pepper, olive and feta rolls

Preparation time:
10 minutes, plus standing

Cooking time:
7–8 minutes

Serves: **4**

2 red peppers, cored, deseeded and quartered lengthways
100 g (3½ oz) feta cheese, thinly sliced or crumbled
16 basil leaves
16 pitted black olives, halved
15 g (½ oz) pine nuts, toasted
1 tablespoon pesto
1 tablespoon French dressing

TO SERVE
rocket leaves
crusty bread

Put the red pepper quarters, skin side up, on a baking sheet and cook under a preheated high grill for 7–8 minutes until the skins are blackened.

Transfer the pepper quarters to a polythene bag. Fold over the top to seal and leave for 10 minutes, then peel away the skins.

Lay the skinned pepper quarters on a board and layer some feta, basil, olives and pine nuts on each one. Carefully roll up each pepper quarter and secure with a cocktail stick. Put 2 pepper rolls on each serving plate.

Whisk the pesto and French dressing together in a small bowl and drizzle over the pepper rolls. Serve with rocket leaves and some crusty bread to mop up the juices.

38 Prawn, mango and avocado wrap

Preparation time:
10 minutes

Cooking time:
No cooking

Serves: **4**

2 tablespoons crème fraîche
2 teaspoons tomato ketchup
a few drops of Tabasco sauce, to taste
300 g (10 oz) cooked peeled prawns
1 mango, peeled, stoned and thinly sliced
1 avocado, peeled, stoned and sliced
100 g (3½ oz) watercress
4 soft flour tortillas

Mix together the crème fraîche, ketchup and Tabasco in a bowl. Add the prawns, mango and avocado and toss gently to mix.

Divide the prawn mixture and the watercress among the tortillas, roll up and serve immediately.

COOK'S NOTES Although this quick and easy starter is simple to prepare, it looks and tastes delicious. Serve the wraps in small bowls or cups for a variation.

39 Asparagus with lemon and anchovy butter

40 Sesame steamed prawns

Preparation time:
10 minutes, plus chilling

Cooking time:
5 minutes

Serves: **4**

50 g (2 oz) drained anchovy fillets in oil
150 g (5 oz) butter, softened
a pinch of chilli powder
juice of 1 lemon, or to taste
1 kg (2 lb) asparagus spears, trimmed
pepper

Put the anchovies, butter, chilli powder and pepper to taste in a blender or food processor and blend until smooth. Add lemon juice to taste. Roll the butter into a log, wrap in foil and chill in the freezer for 15 minutes.

Steam the asparagus in a steamer for 4–5 minutes or until just tender. Meanwhile, remove the butter from the freezer, unwrap it and cut into 1 cm (½ inch) slices.

Serve the asparagus immediately, topped with the slices of butter.

Preparation time:
15 minutes

Cooking time:
5 minutes

Serves: **4**

16 raw tiger prawns, peeled and
**   deveined but tails left intact**
2 garlic cloves, sliced
1 red chilli, deseeded and chopped
finely grated rind and juice of 1 lime
2.5 cm (1 inch) piece of fresh root ginger,
**   peeled and chopped**
2 tablespoons rice wine
2 tablespoons Thai fish sauce
4 Savoy cabbage leaves
1 tablespoon sesame oil
salt
a few fresh coriander, mint and basil
**   leaves, to garnish**

To butterfly the prawns, cut down the deveining slit on the back of each prawn so that it opens up and lies flat, leaving the tail intact. Rinse and pat dry with kitchen paper.

Mix together the garlic, chilli, lime rind and juice, ginger, rice wine and fish sauce in a bowl. Add the prawns and toss well.

Blanch the cabbage leaves in a saucepan of lightly salted boiling water for 30 seconds. Drain, refresh under cold running water, drain again and pat dry with kitchen paper.

Arrange the cabbage leaves in a bamboo steamer and carefully spoon the prawns and marinade on top of the leaves. Cover and steam for 2–3 minutes until the prawns have turned pink.

Meanwhile, heat the oil in a small saucepan. Arrange the cabbage leaves and prawns in a serving dish. Pour the hot oil over them, garnish with the herbs and serve immediately.

COOK'S NOTES You could use 1 tablespoon dried shrimp or 2 tablespoons Thai fish sauce instead of the anchovies if you prefer.

Preparation time: **15 minutes**	**500 g (1 lb) boneless, skinless chicken breasts, cut into 2.5 cm (1 inch) pieces**
Cooking time: **about 15 minutes**	MARINADE **1 tablespoon ground cinnamon** **1 tablespoon ground cumin**
Serves: **4**	**1 teaspoon pepper** **150 ml (¼ pint) groundnut oil** **100 ml (3½ fl oz) soy sauce** **2 tablespoons light muscovado sugar**

SATAY SAUCE
1 heaped teaspoon red Thai curry paste
1 tablespoon groundnut oil
250 ml (8 fl oz) coconut milk
50 g (2 oz) light muscovado sugar
2 tablespoons Thai fish sauce
juice of 1 lime
65 g (2½ oz) crushed unsalted roasted peanuts
1 teaspoon crushed dried red chillies

TO GARNISH
roughly chopped onion
cucumber chunks

Preparation time: **15 minutes**	**4 boneless, skinless chicken breasts, about 150 g (5 oz) each** **6 tablespoons hoisin sauce**
Cooking time: **7 minutes**	TO SERVE **12 Chinese pancakes**
Serves: **4**	**½ cucumber, cut into matchsticks** **12 spring onions, thinly sliced** **handful of fresh coriander** **4 tablespoons hoisin sauce mixed with 3 tablespoons water**

Lay the chicken breasts between 2 sheets of clingfilm or nonstick baking paper and flatten with a rolling pin or meat mallet until they are 2.5 cm (1 inch) thick. Transfer to a baking sheet and brush with some of the hoisin sauce.

Cook the chicken breasts under a preheated high grill for 4 minutes. Turn them over, brush with the remaining hoisin sauce and cook for a further 3 minutes or until the chicken is cooked through. Meanwhile, warm the pancakes in a bamboo steamer for 3 minutes or until heated through.

Thinly slice the chicken and arrange it on a serving plate. Serve with the pancakes, accompanied by the cucumber, spring onions, coriander and diluted hoisin sauce in separate bowls, for everyone to assemble their own pancakes.

Mix all the marinade ingredients together in a bowl. Add the chicken and turn to coat. Cover and leave to marinate in a cool place while you make the sauce.

Put the curry paste in a pan with the oil and stir over a low heat for 1 minute. Add the remaining sauce ingredients and cook over a medium heat until thickened. Turn into a serving bowl and leave to cool.

Thread the chicken on to skewers. Cook under a preheated high grill, in batches, for 2 minutes or until cooked through, turning once. Keep the cooked chicken warm in a low oven while you cook the remainder. Garnish with chopped onion and cucumber and serve with the sauce.

COOK'S NOTES Often served as part of a Chinese meal, this is a time-saving starter as you don't need to put the pancakes together.

43 Haloumi with sun-dried tomatoes

44 Spiced pumpkin with coconut pesto

Preparation time:
10 minutes

Cooking time:
8–10 minutes

Serves: **4**

200 g (7 oz) haloumi cheese, sliced
2 teaspoons onion seeds
1 tablespoon finely chopped fresh
  coriander leaves
a few saffron threads

TO SERVE
20 g (¾ oz) sun-dried tomatoes in oil,
  drained and sliced
½ orange, peeled and pith removed,
  separated into segments
2 tablespoons lemon juice
rocket leaves, to garnish

Lay the cheese slices on a foil-lined grill pan and sprinkle over the onion seeds, coriander leaves and saffron threads.

Cook the cheese under a preheated medium grill for 4–5 minutes on each side until soft and slightly browned.

Serve the cheese immediately on a bed of the sun-dried tomato slices and orange segments. Drizzle the lemon juice over the cheese just before serving and garnish with a few rocket leaves.

Preparation time:
10 minutes

Cooking time:
15–20 minutes

Serves: **4**

1 teaspoon cumin seeds
1 teaspoon coriander seeds
2 green cardamom pods
1 kg (2 lb) pumpkin, cut into 1 cm (½ inch)
  thick wedges
3 tablespoons sunflower oil
1 teaspoon caster sugar

COCONUT PESTO
25 g (1 oz) fresh coriander leaves
1 garlic clove, crushed
1 green chilli, deseeded and chopped
pinch of sugar
1 tablespoon shelled pistachio nuts,
  roughly chopped
6 tablespoons coconut cream
1 tablespoon lime juice
salt and pepper

Heat a nonstick frying pan until hot, add the whole spices and cook over a medium heat, stirring constantly, until lightly browned. Grind to a powder in a spice grinder or in a mortar with a pestle.

Put the pumpkin wedges in a dish. Toss well with the oil, sugar and spice mix to coat evenly. Cook the wedges on a preheated barbecue or under a high grill for 6–8 minutes on each side until charred and tender.

Meanwhile, to make the pesto, put the coriander, garlic, chilli, sugar, pistachio nuts and salt and pepper to taste in a food processor and process until fairly smooth. Add the coconut cream and lime juice and process again. Transfer to a bowl and serve with the pumpkin.

COOK'S NOTES Haloumi makes a good substitute for meat as it has a wonderful coarse texture when grilled. Serve this starter if you have a mixture of vegetarian and meat-eating guests.

45 Tortillas with aubergine and yogurt

46 Provolone cheese and steak panini

Preparation time:	4 tablespoons olive oil
10 minutes	1 aubergine, thinly sliced
	small handful of mint, chopped
Cooking time:	small handful of parsley, chopped
10 minutes	2 tablespoons chopped chives
	1 green chilli, deseeded and thinly sliced
Serves: **2**	200 ml (7 fl oz) Greek yogurt
	2 tablespoons mayonnaise
	2 large soft flour tortillas
	7 cm (3 inch) length of cucumber, thinly sliced
	salt and pepper
	paprika, to garnish

Heat the oil in a frying pan, add the aubergine and cook for 10 minutes or until golden. Remove with a slotted spoon, drain on kitchen paper and leave to cool slightly.

Meanwhile, mix the herbs with the chilli, yogurt and mayonnaise in a bowl and season to taste with salt and pepper.

Arrange the warm aubergine slices over the tortillas and spread with the yogurt mixture. Arrange the cucumber slices on top. Roll up each tortilla, sprinkle with paprika to garnish and serve.

COOK'S NOTES Prepare the yogurt mixture in advance and keep it in the refrigerator until you are ready to assemble the tortillas.

Preparation time:	4 tablespoons olive oil
15 minutes	½ red pepper, cored, deseeded and thinly sliced
Cooking time:	½ green pepper, cored deseeded and thinly sliced
about 15 minutes	1 small onion, halved and thinly sliced
Serves: **2**	300 g (10 oz) rib-eye steak, thinly sliced
	75 g (3 oz) mushrooms, trimmed and sliced
	1 garlic clove, chopped
	75 g (3 oz) provolone cheese, thinly sliced
	2 tablespoons Worcestershire or steak sauce
	4 long slices of French country bread
	1 dill pickle, thinly sliced (optional)
	salt and pepper
	cherry tomatoes, to serve

Heat the oil in a frying pan, add the peppers and onion and cook for 3–4 minutes. Add the steak and cook for 2–3 minutes, then add the mushrooms and garlic and cook for 3–4 minutes.

Reduce the heat to low, season well with salt and pepper and then use 2 wooden spatulas to form the steak mixture into 2 piles, about the size of the bread slices. Lay half the cheese slices on top of each pile and leave to melt for 2 minutes.

Spread a little of the sauce over 2 slices of bread and then very carefully lift the cheese-steak mixture on to the bread, again using 2 spatulas. Splash over the remaining sauce and arrange the pickle slices on top, if using.

Top with the remaining bread slices and toast in a sandwich grill for 2–3 minutes, or according to the manufacturer's instructions, until the bread is crisp and the cheese is completely melted. Serve immediately with a bowl of cherry tomatoes.

Preparation time:
10 minutes

Cooking time:
5 minutes

Serves: **1**

25 g (1 oz) ricotta cheese
½ red onion, thinly sliced
1 tomato, finely chopped
¼ green chilli, finely chopped
1 tablespoon chopped fresh coriander
2 small soft flour tortillas
olive oil, for brushing
green salad, to serve

Mix together the ricotta, onion, tomato, chilli and coriander in a bowl.

Heat a griddle pan until hot. Brush the tortillas with a little oil, add to the pan and cook very briefly on each side.

Spread half the ricotta mixture over one half of each tortilla and fold over the other half to cover. Serve immediately with a green salad.

Preparation time:
8 minutes

Cooking time:
22 minutes

Serves: **2**

Oven temperature:
180°C (350°F) Gas Mark 4

2 boneless, skinless chicken breasts,
about 150 g (5 oz) each
2 teaspoons black olive tapenade
4 sun-dried tomatoes in oil, drained
1 garlic clove, cut into slivers
3–4 rosemary sprigs
2 tablespoons olive oil
2 large wholegrain rolls, halved
horizontally
50 g (2 oz pecorino) cheese, freshly
shaved
salt and pepper
rocket leaves, to garnish

Using a sharp knife, make a horizontal slit in each chicken breast. Do not cut all the way through but just deep enough to create a pocket in the flesh. Divide the tapenade, sun-dried tomatoes and garlic slivers between the pockets and close up.

Lay the chicken breasts on top of the rosemary sprigs in a roasting tin and drizzle with the oil. Season with a little salt and pepper and cook in a preheated oven, 180°C (350°F), Gas Mark 4, for 18 minutes or until the chicken is cooked through.

When the chicken is cool enough to handle, cut it into slices. Arrange the chicken on the wholegrain roll bases, sprinkle with the pecorino shavings and top with the lids. Toast in a sandwich grill for 3–4 minutes, or according to the manufacturer's instructions, until the bread is golden and the chicken is hot. Serve immediately, garnished with rocket leaves.

COOK'S NOTES The ideal snack or lunch dish that is as quick to prepare as a sandwich. If you don't have a griddle pan wrap the tortillas in foil and heat them through in the oven.

49 Goats' cheese and herb soufflés

50 Caesar salad

Preparation time:
10 minutes

Cooking time:
15 minutes

Serves: **4**

Oven temperature:
190°C (375°F) Gas Mark 5

25 g (1 oz) margarine
50 g (2 oz) plain flour
300 ml (½ pint) semi-skimmed milk
4 eggs, separated
100 g (3½ oz) goats' cheese, crumbled
1 tablespoon chopped mixed herbs, such
  as parsley, chives and thyme
vegetable oil, for oiling
1 tablespoon freshly grated Parmesan
  cheese
salt and pepper

TO SERVE
75 g (3 oz) rocket leaves
2 tablespoons French dressing

Preparation time:
20 minutes

Cooking time:
5 minutes

Serves: **4**

1 garlic clove, crushed
4 anchovy fillets in oil, drained and
  chopped
3 tablespoons lemon juice
2 teaspoons English mustard powder
1 egg yolk
200 ml (7 fl oz) extra virgin olive oil
3–4 tablespoons vegetable oil
3 slices of country bread, crusts
  removed, cut into 1 cm (½ inch) dice
1 cos lettuce, torn into pieces
3 tablespoons freshly grated Parmesan
  cheese
pepper

Melt the margarine in a medium saucepan, add the flour and cook, stirring constantly, for 1 minute. Gradually add the milk, whisking constantly, and cook for 2 minutes until thickened.

Remove the pan from the heat. Beat in the egg yolks, one at a time, then stir in the goats' cheese. Season well with salt and pepper.

Whisk the eggs whites in a large bowl until stiff peaks form, then gradually fold them into the cheese mixture with the herbs. Transfer the soufflé mixture to 4 lightly oiled ramekins, sprinkle over the Parmesan and bake in a preheated oven, 190°C (375°F), Gas Mark 5, for 10–12 minutes until risen and golden.

Meanwhile, toss the rocket leaves and dressing together in a bowl. Serve with the soufflés hot from the oven.

Put the garlic, anchovies, lemon juice, mustard and egg yolk in a small bowl and season to taste with pepper. Using a hand-held blender or small electric whisk, blend or beat until well combined. Slowly drizzle in the olive oil, mixing constantly, to form a thick, creamy sauce. If the sauce becomes too thick, add a little water.

Heat the vegetable oil in a heavy-based frying pan, add the bread cubes and cook, turning and stirring frequently, for 5 minutes or until they are golden and crisp all over. Remove them with a slotted spoon and drain on kitchen paper.

Put the lettuce in a large bowl, add the dressing and 2 tablespoons of the Parmesan and mix well.

Serve the salad in a large bowl or on individual plates, sprinkled with the croûtons and the remaining Parmesan.

COOK'S NOTES For a more substantial meal you could add some chicken to the salad. Grill or bake 2 chicken breasts, cut them into long strips and arrange over the other ingredients before serving.

51 Peppered beef with green salad

52 Griddled aubergines with chilli toasts

Preparation time:
20 minutes

Cooking time:
4–7 minutes

Serves: **6**

**2 thick-cut sirloin steaks, about 500 g
   (1 lb) in total**
**3 teaspoons mixed peppercorns, coarsely
   crushed**
2 teaspoons coarse salt flakes
200 ml (7 fl oz) natural yogurt
**1–1½ teaspoons horseradish sauce, to
   taste**
1 garlic clove, crushed
150 g (5 oz) mixed green salad leaves
100 g (3½ oz) button mushrooms, sliced
1 red onion, thinly sliced
1 tablespoon olive oil
salt and pepper

Trim any fat from the steak and rub the meat with the crushed peppercorns and salt flakes.

Mix together the yogurt, horseradish sauce and garlic in a large bowl and season to taste with salt and pepper. Add the salad leaves, mushrooms and most of the onion and toss gently.

Heat the oil in a frying pan, add the steaks and cook over a high heat for 2 minutes until browned. Turn them over and cook for 2 minutes for medium rare, 3–4 minutes for medium or 5 minutes for well done.

Spoon an equal quantity of the salad leaves into the centre of 6 serving plates. Thinly slice the steaks and arrange the slices on top of the leaves, then garnish with the remaining onion.

Preparation time:
15 minutes

Cooking time:
10 minutes

Serves: **4**

Oven temperature:
220°C (425°F) Gas Mark 7

**2 aubergines, about 550 g (1lb 2 oz) in
   total**
2 teaspoons olive oil
50 g (2 oz) sun-blush tomatoes
2 garlic cloves, crushed
4 tablespoons lemon juice
pepper
4 basil leaves, to garnish

CHILLI TOASTS
4 slices of multigrain bread
1 tablespoon chilli oil

To make the chilli toasts, cut the crusts from the bread slices and cut each slice into 2 neat triangles. Brush each side with the chilli oil and arrange on a baking sheet. Bake the chilli toasts in a preheated oven, 220°C (425°F), Gas Mark 7, for 8–10 minutes until crisp and golden.

Meanwhile, cut the aubergines lengthways into 5 mm (¼ inch) slices and season to taste with pepper. Brush a ridged griddle pan with the olive oil and heat until hot. Add the aubergine slices and tomatoes with the garlic and cook for 4 minutes or until starting to soften. Turn the aubergines over and cook for a further 4 minutes. Sprinkle over the lemon juice.

Serve the chilli toasts with the aubergines and tomatoes piled high in the centre of individual serving plates, garnished with basil leaves and pepper.

COOK'S NOTES The quantities given here would also make a main course for two.

53 Parmesan polenta with salsa

54 Tomato and green bean salad

Preparation time:
10 minutes, plus standing

Cooking time:
about 15 minutes

Serves: **4**

75 g (3 oz) quick-cooking polenta
500 ml (17 fl oz) simmering water
75 g (3 oz) butter, plus extra for greasing
40 g (1½ oz) Parmesan cheese, freshly grated
6 tablespoons chopped mixed herbs, such as chervil, chives and parsley
salt and pepper

SALSA
300 g (10 oz) cherry tomatoes, quartered
2 red chillies, deseeded and finely chopped
1 small red onion, finely chopped
2 tablespoons chilli oil
2 tablespoons olive oil
2 tablespoons lime juice
2 tablespoons shredded mint

Pour the polenta into a saucepan of the simmering measured water and beat well with a wooden spoon until thick and smooth. Reduce the heat and cook, stirring constantly, for 6–8 minutes, or according to the packet instructions.

Remove the pan from the heat and stir in the butter, Parmesan, herbs and salt and pepper to taste. Turn the polenta into a greased 25 cm (10 inch) pizza or cake tin at least 2.5 cm (1 inch) deep. Smooth the top and leave to stand for 5 minutes or until set.

Meanwhile, mix all the salsa ingredients together in a bowl. Season to taste with salt and pepper.

Carefully transfer the polenta to a chopping board and cut it into 8 wedges. Heat a griddle pan until hot, add the polenta wedges and cook for 2–3 minutes on each side until heated through and golden. Serve immediately with the salsa.

Preparation time:
10 minutes

Cooking time:
5 minutes

Serves: **4**

250 g (8 oz) mixed red and yellow baby tomatoes, plum if possible
250 g (8 oz) thin green beans, trimmed
handful of mint leaves, chopped
1 garlic clove, crushed and chopped
4 tablespoons extra virgin olive oil
1 tablespoon balsamic vinegar
salt and pepper

Cut the tomatoes in half and put them in a large bowl.

Blanch the beans in a large saucepan of boiling water for 2 minutes. Drain well and add to the tomatoes.

Add the mint, garlic, oil and vinegar. Season to taste with salt and pepper and mix well. Serve warm or cold.

COOK'S NOTES This simple salad is very easy to prepare but the wonderful combination of flavours and colours makes it an attractive and delicious starter. If serving cold, it can be prepared a little in advance.

55 Griddled artichokes and fennel

Preparation time:
15 minutes

Cooking time:
7–8 minutes

Serves: **6**

3 tablespoons olive oil
**3 teaspoons finely chopped rosemary
   leaves**
**200 g (7 oz) fennel, trimmed and cut into
   small wedges**
**400 g (13 oz) can artichoke hearts,
   drained and halved**
100 g (3½ oz) feta cheese, crumbled
rosemary sprigs, to garnish

DRESSING
finely grated rind and juice of 1 lemon
2 teaspoons capers, drained and rinsed
4 teaspoons balsamic vinegar
salt and pepper

Put the oil, chopped rosemary and a little salt and pepper into a polythene bag. Add the fennel and artichoke hearts and shake gently in the bag to coat.

Heat a ridged griddle pan until smoking. Add the dressed vegetables and cook for 3–4 minutes until the undersides are browned. Turn them over and cook for 2 minutes. Crumble the feta over the top, put the pan under a preheated high grill and cook for 2 minutes until the cheese is hot but not melted.

Meanwhile, mix all the dressing ingredients together with any remaining oil in the polythene bag.

Spoon the vegetables on to serving plates and drizzle the dressing over the top. Garnish with extra rosemary leaves torn from the sprigs.

56 Mixed leaf and pomegranate salad

Preparation time:
10 minutes

Cooking time:
No cooking

Serves: **6**

3 tablespoons raspberry vinegar
2 tablespoons light olive oil
1 pomegranate
**125 g (4 oz) mixed salad leaves, including
   baby spinach leaves, red mustard and
   mizuna**
salt and pepper
raspberries, to garnish (optional)

Put the raspberry vinegar, oil and a little salt and pepper in a salad bowl and mix together lightly.

Cut the pomegranate in half, then cut it into large pieces and flex the skin so that the small red seeds fall out. Pick out any stubborn ones with a small knife and discard, then add the remainder to the salad bowl, discarding the skin and pith.

Tear any large salad leaves into bite-sized pieces and toss in the dressing. Sprinkle with raspberries, if you like, and serve immediately.

COOK'S NOTES To save time, squeeze the pomegranate on a lemon juicer to release the seeds.

3 Vegetables and Salads

57 Orange and avocado salad

Preparation time:
15 minutes

Cooking time:
No cooking

Serves: **4**

4 large juicy oranges
2 small ripe avocados, peeled and stoned
2 teaspoons green cardamom pods
3 tablespoons light olive oil
1 tablespoon clear honey
pinch of ground allspice
2 teaspoons lemon juice
salt and pepper
watercress sprigs, to garnish

Remove the peel and pith from the oranges. Working over a bowl to catch the juice, cut between the membranes to remove the segments. Slice the avocados and toss gently with the orange segments. Pile on to serving plates.

Reserve a few whole cardamom pods for garnishing. Put the remainder in a bowl and crush with the end of a rolling pin or put in a mortar and crush with a pestle to extract the seeds. Pick out and discard the pods.

Mix the cardamom seeds with the oil, honey, allspice, lemon juice, salt and pepper to taste and the reserved orange juice.

Garnish the salads with the watercress sprigs and reserved cardamom pods, and serve with the dressing spooned over the top.

COOK'S NOTES The avocados need to be completely ripe for this recipe. If they are a little hard, put them in the airing cupboard for a couple of hours and they should soften.

58 Watermelon and feta salad

Preparation time:
10 minutes

Cooking time:
5 minutes

Serves: **4**

1 tablespoon black sesame seeds
500 g (1 lb) watermelon, peeled, deseeded and diced
175 g (6 oz) feta cheese, diced
75 g (3 oz) rocket leaves
handful of mint, parsley and fresh coriander sprigs
6 tablespoons extra virgin olive oil
1 tablespoon orange flower water
1½ tablespoons lemon juice
1 teaspoon pomegranate syrup (optional)
½ teaspoon sugar
salt and pepper
toasted pitta bread, to serve

Heat a nonstick frying pan, add the sesame seeds and cook, stirring constantly, for 2–3 minutes until lightly browned. Set aside.

Arrange the watermelon and feta on a large plate with the rocket leaves and herbs.

Whisk together the oil, orange flower water, lemon juice, pomegranate syrup, if using, and sugar in a small bowl and season to taste with salt and pepper. Drizzle the dressing over the salad, scatter over the toasted sesame seeds and serve with toasted pitta bread.

COOK'S NOTES Orange flower water is used in a lot of Middle Eastern recipes, both sweet and savoury. You will find it in specialist grocers or larger supermarkets.

59 Papaya and lime salad

60 Asparagus salad

Preparation time:
15 minutes, plus cooling

Cooking time:
5 minutes

Serves: **4**

3 firm ripe papayas
finely grated rind and juice of 2 limes
2 teaspoons soft light brown sugar
50 g (2 oz) blanched almonds, toasted
lime wedges, to decorate

Cut the papayas in half lengthways, scoop out the seeds and discard. Peel the halves, roughly dice the flesh and put it in a bowl.

Finely grate the rind of both limes, then squeeze the juice from one of the limes and reserve. Remove the pith from the other lime. Working over the bowl of papaya to catch the juice, cut between the membranes to remove the segments. Add the lime segments and grated rind to the papaya.

Pour the reserved lime juice into a small saucepan, add the sugar and heat gently until the sugar has dissolved. Remove from the heat and leave to cool for 10 minutes.

Pour the sweetened lime juice over the fruit and toss thoroughly. Add the toasted almonds to the fruit salad, decorate with lime wedges and serve immediately.

Preparation time:
15 minutes

Cooking time:
5–10 minutes

Serves: **4**

3 tablespoons olive oil (optional)
500 g (1 lb) asparagus spears, trimmed
50 g (2 oz) rocket or other salad leaves
2 spring onions, thinly sliced
4 radishes, thinly sliced
salt and pepper
roughly chopped herbs, such as tarragon,
  parsley, chervil and dill, to garnish

DRESSING
finely grated rind of 1 lemon, plus extra
  thin strips to garnish
2 tablespoons tarragon vinegar
1 tablespoon chopped tarragon
¼ teaspoon Dijon mustard
pinch of sugar
5 tablespoons olive oil

To make the dressing, put all the ingredients in a screw-top jar and shake until well blended.

Heat the oil, if using, in a griddle pan. Arrange as many asparagus spears as will fit in a single layer over the base of the pan and cook, turning occasionally, for 5 minutes or until just tender and slightly charred. Transfer to a shallow dish, season to taste with salt and pepper and set aside while you cook the remainder. Pour over the dressing, toss gently to coat evenly and leave to stand for 5 minutes.

Arrange the rocket or other leaves on a platter, scatter the spring onions and radishes over the top and arrange the asparagus in a pile in the centre. Garnish with the chopped herbs and thin strips of lemon rind.

COOK'S NOTES **Papaya and lime complement each other beautifully. This simple but utterly delicious fruit salad can be served for brunch or breakfast with muesli and yogurt, or on its own.**

61 Spring vegetable salad with garlic bread

62 Smoked chicken and avocado salad

Preparation time:
10 minutes

Cooking time:
10 minutes

Serves: **4**

200 g (7 oz) fresh or frozen peas
200 g (7 oz) asparagus spears, trimmed
200 g (7 oz) sugar snap peas
2 courgettes, cut into long thin ribbons
   with a vegetable peeler
1 fennel bulb, trimmed and very thinly
   sliced
finely grated rind and juice of 1 lemon
1 teaspoon Dijon mustard
1 teaspoon clear honey
1 tablespoon chopped parsley
2 tablespoons olive oil

GARLIC BREAD
4 ciabatta rolls, halved horizontally
1 garlic clove, peeled but left whole

Preparation time:
15 minutes

Cooking time:
5 minutes

Serves: **4**

5 tablespoons extra virgin olive oil
4 slices of day-old bread, crusts
   removed, cut into 1 cm (½ inch) dice
500 g (1 lb) cold cooked smoked chicken
   breast, sliced
3 Little Gem or baby cos lettuce hearts
1 large ripe avocado, peeled, stoned and
   diced
25 g (1 oz) Parmesan cheese, freshly
   grated

DRESSING
125 ml (4 fl oz) extra virgin olive oil
2 tablespoons tarragon vinegar
1 tablespoon wholegrain mustard
1 tablespoon chopped tarragon
1 teaspoon caster sugar
salt and pepper

Blanch the peas, asparagus and sugar snap peas in a large saucepan of boiling water for 3 minutes. Drain, refresh under cold running water and drain again.

Transfer the vegetables to a large bowl with the courgette ribbons and fennel and mix together.

Whisk together the lemon rind and juice, mustard, honey, parsley and half the oil in a small bowl. Toss the dressing through the vegetables.

Rub the cut sides of the rolls with the garlic, drizzle over the remaining oil, then place the rolls on a baking sheet and toast on both sides under a preheated high grill. Serve with the vegetables.

To make the croûtons, heat the oil in a heavy-based frying pan, add the bread cubes and cook, turning and stirring frequently, for 5 minutes or until golden and crisp all over. Remove with a slotted spoon and drain on kitchen paper.

Cut the chicken breast slices into bite-sized pieces and put in a large bowl. Separate the lettuce leaves and add to the chicken with the avocado, croûtons and Parmesan.

Whisk together all the dressing ingredients in a small bowl and season to taste with salt and pepper. Pour the dressing over the salad and toss well to coat evenly. Serve immediately.

COOK'S NOTES Because smoked chicken is hot-smoked, it is already cooked and ready to eat. If you are especially short of time, you can buy ready-made croûtons, but it is easy to make your own.

63 Italian broccoli and egg salad

Preparation time:
10 minutes

Cooking time:
10 minutes

Serves: **4**

4 eggs
300 g (10 oz) broccoli
2 small leeks, about 300 g (10 oz)
4 tablespoons lemon juice
2 tablespoons olive oil
2 teaspoons clear honey
1 tablespoon capers, drained and rinsed
**2 tablespoons chopped tarragon, plus
  extra sprigs to garnish (optional)**
salt and pepper
wholemeal bread, to serve

Half-fill the base of a steamer with water, add the eggs and bring to the boil. Cover with the steamer top and simmer for 8 minutes until hard-boiled.

Meanwhile, cut the broccoli into florets and thickly slice the broccoli stems and the leeks. Add the broccoli to the top of the steamer and steam for 3 minutes. Add the leeks and steam for a further 2 minutes.

Mix together the oil, honey, capers and tarragon in a salad bowl to make the dressing.

Crack the hard-boiled eggs, cool quickly under cold running water, then shell and roughly chop the eggs.

Add the broccoli and leeks to the dressing, toss together and sprinkle with the chopped eggs. Garnish with tarragon sprigs, if you like, and serve warm with thickly sliced wholemeal bread.

64 Spinach, Gorgonzola and walnut salad

Preparation time:
10 minutes, plus cooling

Cooking time:
5 minutes

Serves: **4**

1 tablespoon clear honey
125 g (4 oz) walnut halves
250 g (8 oz) green beans, trimmed
200 g (7 oz) baby spinach leaves
150 g (5 oz) Gorgonzola, crumbled

DRESSING
4 tablespoons walnut oil
2 tablespoons extra virgin olive oil
1–2 tablespoons sherry vinegar
salt and pepper

Heat the honey in a small frying pan, add the walnuts and cook over a medium heat, stirring, for 2–3 minutes until the nuts are glazed. Tip on to a plate and leave to cool until required.

Meanwhile, blanch the beans in a saucepan of lightly salted boiling water for 3 minutes. Drain, refresh under cold running water, drain again and shake dry. Put in a large bowl with the spinach leaves.

Whisk together all the dressing ingredients in a small bowl and season to taste with salt and pepper. Pour over the salad and toss well to coat evenly. Arrange the salad in bowls, scatter over the Gorgonzola and honeyed walnuts and serve immediately.

COOK'S NOTES Gorgonzola has a strong, piquant taste and creamy texture. If you prefer a milder blue cheese flavour, use dolcelatte instead.

65 Chickpea and olive salad

66 Bulgar wheat salad

Preparation time:
10 minutes

Cooking time:
No cooking

Serves: **4**

**200 g (7 oz) can chickpeas, drained and
  rinsed**
50 g (2 oz) pitted black olives, halved
½ red onion, finely chopped
150 g (5 oz) cherry tomatoes, halved
**3 tablespoons chopped flat leaf parsley,
  plus extra to garnish**
50 g (2 oz) watercress, to serve

DRESSING
1 garlic clove, crushed
100 ml (3½ fl oz) Greek yogurt
juice of ½ lime
pepper

To make the dressing, mix together the garlic, yogurt and lime juice in a small bowl. Season to taste with pepper.

Mix together the chickpeas, olives, onion, tomatoes and parsley in a large bowl.

Add the dressing to the chickpea mixture and toss well to coat evenly. Serve the salad on a bed of watercress, garnished with chopped parsley.

Preparation:
15 minutes, plus soaking

Cooking time:
about 10 minutes

Serves: **4**

150 g (5 oz) bulgar wheat
2 tablespoons olive oil
2 fennel bulbs, trimmed and thinly sliced
175 g (6 oz) baby spinach leaves
**3 oranges, peel and pith removed,
  separated into segments**
2 tablespoons pumpkin seeds, toasted

DRESSING
4 tablespoons natural yogurt
2 tablespoons chopped fresh coriander
½ small cucumber, finely chopped
salt (optional) and pepper

Put the bulgar wheat in a heatproof bowl, cover with plenty of boiling water and leave to soak for 15 minutes.

Meanwhile, heat half the oil in a frying pan, add the fennel and cook for 8–10 minutes until tender and browned. Add the spinach and cook, stirring, until just wilted. Remove from the heat.

Drain the bulgar wheat thoroughly in a sieve, pressing out as much moisture as possible with the back of a spoon. Add to the pan and toss well to mix, then add the orange segments and pumpkin seeds.

Mix together all the dressing ingredients with the remaining oil in a small bowl, stir through the salad and serve.

COOK'S NOTES This is a very simple salad that uses mainly store-cupboard ingredients. You can substitute regular tomatoes for cherry and, if you don't have watercress, other salad leaves, such as rocket, will work equally well.

67 Spiced couscous salad

Preparation time:	200 ml (7 fl oz) vegetable stock
10 minutes, plus standing	200 ml (7 fl oz) orange juice
	1 teaspoon ground cinnamon
Cooking time:	½ teaspoon ground coriander
3 minutes	250 g (8 oz) couscous
	75 g (3 oz) raisins
Serves: **4**	2 tomatoes, chopped
	¼ preserved lemon, chopped (optional)
	½ bunch of parsley, roughly chopped
	½ bunch of mint, roughly chopped
	1 garlic clove, crushed
	4 tablespoons extra virgin olive oil
	salt and pepper

Mix together the stock, orange juice, spices and ½ teaspoon salt in a saucepan. Bring to the boil and stir in the couscous. Remove from the heat, cover and leave to stand for 10 minutes until all the liquid has been absorbed.

Mix together the raisins, tomatoes, preserved lemon, if using, herbs, garlic and oil in a large bowl, stir in the soaked couscous and season to taste with salt and pepper.

Serve warm or leave to cool and serve at room temperature.

68 Tabbouleh with fruit and nuts

Preparation time:	150 g (5 oz) bulgar wheat
15 minutes, plus soaking	75 g (3 oz) unsalted shelled pistachio nuts
Cooking time:	1 small red onion, finely chopped
No cooking	3 garlic cloves, crushed
	25 g (1 oz) flat leaf parsley, chopped
Serves: **4**	15 g (½ oz) mint, chopped
	finely grated rind and juice of 1 lemon or lime
	150 g (5 oz) ready-to-eat prunes, sliced
	4 tablespoons olive oil
	salt and pepper

Put the bulgar wheat in a heatproof bowl, cover with plenty of boiling water and leave to soak for 15 minutes.

Meanwhile, put the pistachio nuts in a separate heatproof bowl and cover with boiling water. Leave to stand for 1 minute, then drain. Rub the nuts between several thicknesses of kitchen paper to remove most of the skins, then peel away any remaining skins with your fingers.

Mix the nuts with the onion, garlic, parsley, mint, lemon or lime rind and juice and prunes in a large bowl.

Drain the bulgar wheat thoroughly in a sieve, pressing out as much moisture as possible with the back of a spoon. Add to the bowl with the oil and toss together. Season to taste with salt and pepper and serve.

COOK'S NOTES Couscous has a light, fluffy texture and makes a perfect base for salads. The varieties readily available in supermarkets are generally pre-prepared and need only to be soaked in boiling water, but double check the packet instructions, because some types need longer cooking times.

Preparation time:
10 minutes

Cooking time:
No cooking

Serves: **1**

100 g (3½ oz) cold cooked chicken breast, sliced
75 g (3 oz) mixed black and green grapes, halved
1 head of chicory
handful of watercress
bread, to serve

DRESSING
1 teaspoon clear honey
½ teaspoon Dijon mustard
1 tablespoon crème fraîche
pepper

Put the chicken and grapes in a salad bowl. Separate the chicory into leaves and break the watercress into small sprigs. Add the chicory and watercress to the bowl and toss the ingredients together.

To make the dressing, put all the ingredients in a small bowl, season to taste with pepper and whisk well.

Pour the dressing over the salad and toss well to coat evenly. Serve with a slice of bread.

Preparation time:
10 minutes, plus resting

Cooking time:
about 10 minutes

Serves: **4**

2 lean rump or sirloin steaks, about 150 g (5 oz) each, trimmed of fat
150 g (5 oz) baby corn cobs
1 large cucumber
1 small red onion, finely chopped
3 tablespoons chopped fresh coriander
4 tablespoons rice vinegar
4 tablespoons sweet chilli sauce
2 tablespoons sesame seeds, lightly toasted

Heat a griddle pan until smoking, add the steaks and cook for 3–4 minutes on each side. Remove the steaks from the pan and leave to rest for 10 minutes, then thinly slice.

Meanwhile, blanch the baby corn in a saucepan of boiling water for 3–4 minutes. Drain, refresh under cold running water and drain again thoroughly.

Slice the cucumber in half lengthways, then scoop out and discard the seeds with a teaspoon. Cut the cucumber into 5 mm (¼ inch) slices.

Put the beef, baby corn, cucumber, onion and coriander in a large bowl. Stir in the vinegar and sweet chilli sauce and mix together well. Garnish the salad with the sesame seeds and serve immediately.

COOK'S NOTES This is a great way of using up leftover chicken from a Sunday roast. The sweetness of the grapes combines well with the crisp, fresh flavour of the chicory.

71 Spiced chicken and mango salad

72 Turkey and avocado salad

Preparation time: **15 minutes**	**4 boneless, skinless chicken breasts, about 150 g (5 oz) each** **6 teaspoons mild curry paste**
Cooking time: **5 minutes**	**juice of 1 lemon** **150 ml (¼ pint) natural yogurt** **1 mango**
Serves: **4**	**50 g (2 oz) watercress, torn into bite-sized pieces** **½ cucumber, diced** **½ red onion, chopped** **½ iceberg lettuce**

Cut the chicken breasts into long, thin slices. Put 4 teaspoons of the curry paste in a polythene bag with the lemon juice and mix together by squeezing the bag. Add the chicken and shake gently in the bag to coat.

Half-fill the base of a steamer with water and bring to the boil. Put the chicken in the top of the steamer in a single layer, cover and steam for 5 minutes until thoroughly cooked – the juices should run clear when pierced with a knife.

Meanwhile, mix the remaining curry paste with the yogurt in a bowl. Cut a thick slice off either side of the mango to reveal the large, flat stone. Trim the flesh away from the stone, then remove the skin and cut the flesh into bite-sized chunks. Add the mango to the yogurt mixture with the watercress, cucumber and onion and toss together gently.

Tear the lettuce into pieces and divide among 4 plates. Spoon the mango mixture on top and add the warm chicken strips.

Preparation time: **10 minutes**	**350 g (12 oz) cold cooked turkey, sliced** **1 large avocado, peeled, stoned and sliced**
Cooking time: **No cooking**	**1 punnet of mustard and cress** **150 g (5 oz) mixed salad leaves** **50 g (2 oz) mixed seeds, such as pumpkin and sunflower, toasted**
Serves: **4**	**wholegrain rye bread, toasted, or flatbreads, to serve**

DRESSING
2 tablespoons apple juice
2 tablespoons natural yogurt
1 teaspoon clear honey
1 teaspoon wholegrain mustard

Toss together all the salad ingredients and seeds in a large bowl.

Whisk together all the dressing ingredients in a small bowl. Pour over the salad and toss well to coat evenly.

Serve the salad with toasted wholegrain rye bread or rolled up in flatbreads.

COOK'S NOTES To remove the stone from an avocado, slice around the circumference with a sharp knife. Twist the halves until they separate and hold the half with the stone. Very carefully tap the middle of the stone with the blade of the knife and then lift it out – the stone should come too.

73 Panzanella

74 Fig, mozzarella and prosciutto salad

Preparation time: **10 minutes, plus standing**	**3 red peppers, cored, deseeded and quartered lengthways** **375 g (12 oz) plum tomatoes, skinned**
Cooking time: **7–8 minutes**	**6 tablespoons extra virgin olive oil** **3 tablespoons white wine vinegar** **2 garlic cloves, crushed**
Serves: **4**	**125 g (4 oz) stale ciabatta bread** **50 g (2 oz) pitted black olives** **small handful of basil leaves, shredded** **salt and pepper**

Put the red peppers, skin side up, on a baking sheet and cook under a preheated high grill for 7–8 minutes until the skins are blackened.

Transfer the pepper quarters to a polythene bag. Fold over the top to seal and leave for 10 minutes.

Meanwhile, quarter the tomatoes, scoop out the pulp and put it in a sieve over a bowl to catch the juice. Set the tomato quarters aside. Press the pulp with the back of a spoon to extract as much juice as possible. Whisk the oil, vinegar, garlic and salt and pepper to taste into the tomato juice.

Peel away the skins from the peppers. Roughly slice the flesh and put it in a bowl with the tomato quarters. Break the bread into small chunks and add to the bowl with the olives and basil.

Add the dressing and toss the ingredients together before serving.

Preparation time: **10 minutes**	**8–12 ripe figs** **250 g (8 oz) buffalo mozzarella** **8 slices of prosciutto**
Cooking time: **No cooking**	**a few basil leaves**
Serves: **4**	DRESSING **3 tablespoons extra virgin olive oil** **1 tablespoon verjuice** **salt and pepper**

Cut the figs into quarters, tear the mozzarella and prosciutto into bite-sized pieces and arrange on a large platter with the basil leaves.

Whisk together the oil and verjuice in a small bowl and season to taste with salt and pepper. Drizzle over the salad and serve immediately.

COOK'S NOTES Verjuice, made from unripe grapes, has a strong, acidic flavour and is used in cooking as an alternative to lemon juice or vinegar. It gives the dressing a lovely flavour, but if you cannot find it, use a good quality white wine vinegar sweetened with a pinch of sugar.

75 Avocado and smoked salmon salad

76 Hot chicken liver salad

Preparation time:	**2 slices of smoked salmon, about 100 g**
10 minutes	**(3½ oz) each**
	1 small firm avocado, peeled, stoned and
Cooking time:	**cut into wedges**
No cooking	**juice of ½ lime**
	2 teaspoons mayonnaise
Serves: **2**	**1 teaspoon wholegrain mustard**
	2 tablespoons chopped dill
	TO SERVE
	25 g (1 oz) rocket leaves
	2 teaspoons sunflower seeds

Wrap the smoked salmon slices around the avocado wedges and sprinkle with the lime juice.

Mix together the mayonnaise, mustard and dill in a small bowl.

Serve the wrapped avocado on a bed of rocket leaves with the mustard mayonnaise and sprinkled with the sunflower seeds.

Preparation time:	**2 teaspoons chopped thyme leaves**
10 minutes	**400 g (13 oz) chicken livers, trimmed and**
	halved
Cooking time:	**1 tablespoon olive oil**
5 minutes	**2 garlic cloves, crushed**
	1 red chilli, deseeded and thinly sliced
Serves: **4**	**(optional)**
	200 g (7 oz) can water chestnuts, drained
	and halved
	TO SERVE
	200 g (7 oz) chicory, leaves separated
	1½–2 tablespoons balsamic vinegar

Sprinkle the thyme over both sides of the chicken livers.

Heat the oil in a large frying pan, add the garlic and chilli, if using, and cook, stirring, for 30 seconds, then add the chicken livers and water chestnuts. Cook over a medium heat for 3–4 minutes until the livers are browned on the outside but still slightly pink inside.

Serve the chicken livers on a bed of chicory leaves, drizzled with the vinegar and the pan juices.

COOK'S NOTES This is a speedy salad that would work well as a starter as there is hardly any preparation. It is also a healthy option, with the smoked salmon, avocado and sunflower seeds, which are packed full of vitamins and minerals.

77 Chorizo with broad beans

78 Cavolo nero with pancetta

Preparation time:
10 minutes

Cooking time:
10 minutes

Serves: **4–6**

250 g (8 oz) shelled young broad beans
1 tablespoon extra virgin olive oil
2 garlic cloves, roughly chopped
125 g (4 oz) chorizo sausage, cut into
   5 mm (¼ inch) thick slices
1 tablespoon chopped dill
1 tablespoon chopped mint
2 tablespoons lemon juice
salt and pepper
crusty bread, to serve

Preparation time:
10 minutes

Cooking time:
10 minutes

Serves: **4**

1 tablespoon olive oil
1 onion, sliced
1 garlic clove, crushed
1 red chilli, deseeded and diced
125 g (4 oz) pancetta, diced
1 head of cavolo nero
75 ml (3 fl oz) chicken stock
75 g (3 oz) Parmesan cheese, freshly
   coarsely grated
salt and pepper

Blanch the beans in a saucepan of lightly salted boiling water for 1 minute. Drain, rinse under cold running water and drain again. Pat dry with kitchen paper.

Heat the oil in a frying pan, add the garlic and cook gently for 2–3 minutes until softened, then discard. Increase the heat, add the chorizo and cook, stirring, for 2–3 minutes until golden and some of its oil has been released.

Stir in the beans and cook for a further 2–3 minutes, then add the herbs and lemon juice and season to taste with salt and pepper. Mix well. Serve warm with crusty bread.

Heat the oil in a large saucepan, add the onion, garlic, chilli and pancetta and cook for 5 minutes or until the onion is softened.

Meanwhile, trim any wilting leaves from the cavolo nero, then cut the head in half lengthways. Remove and discard the hard central stem and roughly chop the leaves.

Add the cavolo nero to the onion mixture and stir well. Pour in the stock and season to taste with salt and pepper. Cook over a medium heat, stirring constantly, for 4 minutes.

Stir in the Parmesan and serve immediately.

COOK'S NOTES If you want to save time and avoid shelling beans you can use frozen broad beans. They work really well in this recipe as they cut through the rich flavour of the chorizo.

79 Aubergine salad

Preparation time:
10 minutes, plus cooling

Cooking time:
15 minutes

Serves: **4**

4 tablespoons olive oil
1 onion, chopped
2 garlic cloves, crushed
2 aubergines, cubed
4 tomatoes, skinned and roughly chopped
4 anchovy fillets in oil, drained and chopped
2 tablespoons pitted black olives
75 g (3 oz) pine nuts, toasted
2 tablespoons chopped capers
handful of flat leaf parsley, chopped
salt and pepper

DRESSING
1 tablespoon white wine vinegar
3 tablespoons olive oil
2 tablespoons lemon juice
1 teaspoon Dijon mustard

Heat the oil in a saucepan, add the onion, garlic and aubergines and cook for 15 minutes.

Meanwhile, to make the dressing, put all the ingredients in a screw-top jar, season to taste with salt and pepper and shake until well blended.

Add the tomatoes, anchovies, olives, pine nuts, capers and parsley to the aubergine mixture and season to taste with salt and pepper. Pour over the dressing, mix well, then leave the salad to cool for 5 minutes before serving.

COOK'S NOTES Aubergines contain a lot of moisture and you can remove this by placing the chopped aubergines on a large plate and sprinkling them with salt. Leave for about 30 minutes then rinse, or drain on kitchen paper, before using.

80 Bean, kabanos and red pepper salad

Preparation time:
10 minutes, plus standing

Cooking time:
about 15 minutes

Serves: **4**

3 red peppers, cored, deseeded and quartered lengthways
1 red chilli, halved and deseeded
1 tablespoon olive oil
1 onion, sliced
75 g (3 oz) kabanos sausage, thinly sliced
2 x 400 g (13 oz) cans butter or flageolet beans, drained and rinsed
1 tablespoon balsamic vinegar
2 tablespoons chopped fresh coriander
walnut bread, to serve

Put the red pepper quarters and chilli halves, skin-side up, on a baking sheet and cook under a preheated high grill for 7–8 minutes until the skins are blackened.

Transfer the pepper quarters and chilli halves to a polythene bag. Fold over the top to seal and leave for 10 minutes, then peel away the skins and slice the flesh.

Meanwhile, heat the oil in a nonstick frying pan, add the onion and cook for 5–6 minutes until softened. Add the kabanos sausage and cook for 1–2 minutes until crisp.

Add the beans, vinegar and coriander with the peppers and chilli and mix well. Serve the salad warm with walnut bread.

Preparation time:
15 minutes

Cooking time:
10 minutes

Serves: **4**

500 g (1 lb) celeriac, peeled
375 g (12 oz) potatoes, peeled
1 tablespoon extra virgin olive oil, plus
  extra for drizzling (optional)
500 g (1 lb) asparagus spears, trimmed

SAUCE
150 ml (¼ pint) mayonnaise
150 ml (¼ pint) Greek yogurt
1 teaspoon Dijon mustard
6 cocktail gherkins, finely chopped
2 tablespoons capers, chopped
2 tablespoons chopped tarragon
salt and pepper

Cut the celeriac and potato into matchstick-sized pieces, but keep the 2 vegetables separate.

Bring a saucepan of lightly salted water to the boil, add the celeriac and cook for 2 minutes until softened. Add the potatoes and cook for 2 minutes until just tender. Drain the vegetables, refresh under cold running water and drain again.

Meanwhile, thoroughly mix together all the ingredients for the sauce in a bowl and set aside.

Heat the oil in a frying pan or griddle pan, add the asparagus spears and cook for 2–3 minutes until just beginning to colour.

Mix the celeriac and potato with the sauce and spoon on to 4 serving plates. Top with the asparagus and serve immediately, drizzled with a little extra oil, if you like.

COOK'S NOTES This piquant sauce can be used to accompany other salads. It could also be used as a sauce for fish or even as a dip to serve with vegetable crudités.

Preparation time:
15 minutes

Cooking time:
about 15 minutes

Serves: **2**

1 potato, about 175 g (6 oz), scrubbed
1 red pepper, cored, deseeded and sliced
1 teaspoon olive oil
paprika
rock salt

YOGURT DIP
3 tablespoons Greek yogurt
1 tablespoon chopped parsley
2 spring onions, chopped
1 garlic clove, crushed (optional)
salt and pepper

Cut the potato into 8 wedges. Bring a saucepan of lightly salted water to the boil, add the potato wedges and cook for 5 minutes. Drain the wedges thoroughly, then put them in a bowl with the red pepper slices and oil. Toss well to mix. Sprinkle with paprika and rock salt to taste.

Put the potato wedges and pepper slices on a baking sheet and cook under a preheated high grill, turning occasionally, for 6–8 minutes until lightly browned and tender.

Meanwhile, to make the yogurt dip, put all the ingredients in a bowl, season to taste with salt and pepper and mix together well.

Serve the potato wedges and pepper slices hot with the yogurt dip.

COOK'S NOTES For a buffet party dish double the quantities and serve the wedges on a platter for guests to help themselves. You could also try using sweet potatoes for a variation.

83 Charred leek salad with hazelnuts

84 Spiced beetroot

Preparation time:
10 minutes

Cooking time:
15 minutes

Serves: **4**

500 g (1 lb) baby leeks
1–2 tablespoons hazelnut oil
dash of lemon juice
40 g (1½ oz) blanched hazelnuts
2 Little Gem or baby cos lettuce hearts
a few mint sprigs
15 g (½ oz) pecorino cheese
20 black olives, to garnish

DRESSING
4 tablespoons hazelnut oil
2 tablespoons extra virgin olive oil
2 teaspoons sherry vinegar
salt and pepper

Preparation time:
10 minutes

Cooking time:
4–6 minutes

Serves: **4**

1 tablespoon vegetable oil
2 garlic cloves, finely chopped
1 teaspoon grated fresh root ginger
1 teaspoon cumin seeds
1 teaspoon coriander seeds, coarsely crushed
½ teaspoon dried red chilli flakes
625 g (1¼ lb) cooked beetroot in natural juices, drained and cut into wedges
150 ml (¼ pint) canned coconut milk
¼ teaspoon ground cardamom
finely grated rind and juice of 1 lime
handful of chopped fresh coriander leaves
salt and pepper

Brush the leeks with the hazelnut oil to taste and cook in a preheated griddle pan or under a preheated high grill, turning frequently, for 6–8 minutes until evenly browned and cooked through. Transfer the leeks to a bowl, toss with the lemon juice and season to taste with salt and pepper. Leave to cool.

Meanwhile, heat a nonstick frying pan, add the hazelnuts and cook, stirring constantly, for 4–5 minutes until lightly browned. Remove the nuts from the pan and leave to cool slightly, then roughly chop. Separate the lettuce leaves and pull the mint leaves from their stalks.

Arrange the leeks in bowls or on plates and top with the lettuce leaves, mint and nuts.

Whisk together all the dressing ingredients in a small bowl and pour over the salad. Shave the pecorino over the salad and serve immediately, garnished with the olives.

Heat the oil in a wok or large frying pan, add the garlic, ginger, cumin and coriander seeds and chilli flakes and stir-fry for 1–2 minutes. Add the beetroot and cook, stirring gently, for 1 minute. Add the coconut milk, cardamom and lime rind and juice and cook over a medium heat for 2–3 minutes.

Stir in the fresh coriander, season to taste with salt and pepper and serve hot, warm or at room temperature.

COOK'S NOTES Cooked fresh beetroot is now available everywhere; do not use beetroot that has been preserved or cooked in vinegar.

85 Ginger broccoli with fennel seeds

Preparation time:
5 minutes

Cooking time:
5 minutes

Serves: **4**

2 teaspoons olive oil
1 teaspoon crushed fresh root ginger
½ teaspoon fennel seeds
500 g (1 lb) broccoli florets
3 tablespoons soy sauce
pepper

Heat the oil in a nonstick wok or large frying pan, add the ginger and fennel seeds and stir-fry over a medium heat for a few seconds.

Add the broccoli, soy sauce and pepper to taste and stir-fry until the broccoli is just tender. Serve immediately.

86 Pumpkin with walnut and rocket pesto

Preparation time:
10 minutes

Cooking time:
20 minutes

Serves: **4**

Oven temperature:
220°C (425°F) Gas Mark 7

1 kg (2 lb) pumpkin
extra virgin olive oil, for brushing
salt and pepper
rocket leaves, to serve

PESTO
50 g (2 oz) walnuts, toasted
2 spring onions, chopped
1 large garlic clove, crushed
50 g (2 oz) rocket leaves
3 tablespoons walnut oil
3 tablespoons extra virgin olive oil

Cut the pumpkin into 8 wedges and remove and discard the seeds, but leave the skin on. Brush the pumpkin with oil, season to taste with salt and pepper and arrange on a large baking sheet. Roast in a preheated oven, 220°C (425°F), Gas Mark 7, for 20 minutes or until tender, turning it over halfway through.

Meanwhile, to make the pesto, put the walnuts, spring onions, garlic and rocket leaves in a food processor and process until finely chopped. With the machine running, very slowly drizzle in the oils until completely incorporated. Season to taste with salt and pepper.

Serve the roasted pumpkin with the pesto and rocket leaves.

COOK'S NOTES Choose a small, round pumpkin to make cutting easier. Any leftover pesto can be stored in an airtight container in the refrigerator for up to 5 days and tossed with spaghetti for a quick and simple supper dish.

87 Potatoes wrapped in Parma ham

88 Sesame greens with black bean sauce

Preparation time:
10 minutes

Cooking time:
20 minutes

Serves: **4**

Oven temperature:
200°C (400°F) Gas Mark 6

**12 small new potatoes, cooked until just
   tender
12 very thin slices of Parma ham
2 tablespoons olive oil
sea salt**

Roll each potato in a slice of Parma ham, patting with your hands to mould the ham to the shape of the potato.

Brush a roasting tin with the oil, add the potatoes and roast in a preheated oven, 200°C (400°F), Gas Mark 6, for 20 minutes. Keep an eye on the potatoes while they are cooking as they may need turning or moving around; often the ones on the edge become browner than the ones in the centre.

Serve immediately, sprinkled with sea salt to taste.

Preparation time:
10 minutes

Cooking time:
about 10 minutes

Serves: **6**

**5 teaspoons sunflower oil
2 tablespoons sesame seeds
1 tablespoon soy sauce
400 g (13 oz) spring greens or a mix
   of spring greens and Brussels
   sprouts tops
1–2 garlic cloves, finely chopped
3 tablespoons black bean sauce**

Heat 1 teaspoon of the oil in a large frying pan, add the sesame seeds and cook, stirring, for 2–3 minutes, until lightly browned. Remove the pan from the heat, add the soy sauce and quickly cover. When the seeds have stopped popping, stir, recover and leave to cool while you prepare the greens.

Trim the spring greens and discard the stems. Thickly slice the leaves and rinse in cold water. Drain well and pat dry with kitchen paper.

Tip the seeds out of the pan, wash and dry the pan, then add the remaining oil and heat. Add the greens and garlic and stir-fry for 2–3 minutes until just tender. Stir in the black bean sauce and cook for 1 minute. Sprinkle with the toasted sesame seeds, transfer to a serving dish and serve immediately.

COOK'S NOTES You can toss the cooked greens with 1 tablespoon soy sauce instead of the black bean sauce.

89 Asparagus with toasted sesame seeds

90 Tomato and aubergine parmigiana

Preparation time: **10 minutes**	**500 g (1 lb) asparagus spears** **1 tablespoon olive oil** **25 g (1 oz) butter**
Cooking time: **about 15 minutes**	**4 teaspoons sesame seeds** **1 teaspoon wholegrain mustard**
Serves: **6**	

Snap off any woody parts of the asparagus stems by bending the ends of the spears.

Heat the oil and butter in a flat, heavy-based frying pan. Arrange as many asparagus spears as will fit in a single layer over the base of the pan and cook, turning occasionally, for 5 minutes or until just tender and slightly charred. Transfer to a warmed serving dish and keep warm in a low oven while you cook the remainder.

Meanwhile, heat a nonstick frying pan, add the sesame seeds and cook, stirring constantly, for 2–3 minutes until lightly browned.

Stir the mustard into the asparagus and serve immediately, topped with the toasted sesame seeds.

Preparation time: **10 minutes**	**olive oil, for frying** **1 large aubergine, thinly sliced** **500 g (1 lb) ripe plum tomatoes, cut into**
Cooking time: **20 minutes**	**wedges** **50 g (2 oz) Parmesan cheese, freshly** **grated**
Serves: **4**	**salt and pepper** **sprigs of flat leaf parsley, to garnish**
Oven temperature: **190°C (375°F) Gas Mark 5**	

Heat the olive oil in a large, heavy-based frying pan and fry the aubergine slices in batches until golden brown. Drain on kitchen paper.

Arrange the tomato wedges and the fried aubergine slices in alternate layers in a shallow ovenproof dish, with a sprinkling of grated Parmesan between each layer. Season with salt and pepper. Bake in a preheated oven, 190°C (375°F), Gas Mark 5, for 15 minutes, until lightly browned and bubbling.

Allow the vegetables to cool slightly and serve garnished with parsley.

COOK'S NOTES If you're not sure how much of the asparagus stalks to remove, simply hold each spear with one hand at either end, then gently bend: the stalk will give way and break at the right place.

91 Balsamic braised leeks and peppers

Preparation time:
5 minutes

Cooking time:
20 minutes

Serves: **4**

2 tablespoons olive oil
2 leeks, cut into 1 cm (½ inch) pieces
1 orange pepper, cored, deseeded and
** cut into 1 cm (½ inch) chunks**
1 red pepper, cored, deseeded and cut
** into 1 cm (½ inch) chunks**
3 tablespoons balsamic vinegar
handful of flat leaf parsley, chopped
salt and pepper

Heat the oil in a saucepan, add the leeks and peppers and stir well. Cover and cook very gently for 10 minutes.

Add the vinegar and cook, uncovered, for a further 10 minutes. The vegetables should be brown from the vinegar and all the liquid should have evaporated.

Season well with salt and pepper, then stir in the parsley and serve immediately.

92 Warm courgette and lime salad

Preparation time:
10 minutes

Cooking time:
8 minutes

Serves: **4**

1 tablespoon olive oil
finely grated rind and juice of 1 lime
1 garlic clove, finely chopped
2 tablespoons roughly chopped fresh
** coriander leaves, plus extra to garnish**
2 courgettes, about 325 g (11 oz) in total,
** cut into thin diagonal slices**
salt and pepper

Put the oil, lime rind and juice, garlic, coriander and a little salt and pepper in a polythene bag. Add the courgettes and shake gently in the bag to coat. Seal and set aside until ready to cook.

Heat a ridged frying pan until smoking. Arrange as many courgette slices as will fit in a single layer over the base of the pan and cook for 2–3 minutes until the undersides are browned. Turn the courgettes over and brown on the other side, then transfer them to a warmed serving dish while you cook the remainder.

Pour any remaining dressing over the courgettes, sprinkle with chopped coriander to garnish and serve immediately.

COOK'S NOTES As an alternative, you can cook thin slices of aubergine in the same way.

4 Pizza, Pasta, Rice and Noodles

Preparation time:
10 minutes

Cooking time:
15–20 minutes

Serves: **4**

Oven temperature:
230°C (450°F) Gas Mark 8

250 g (8 oz) self-raising flour, plus extra for dusting
3 tablespoons olive oil, plus extra for oiling
1 teaspoon salt
2 tablespoons sun-dried tomato paste
100 ml (3½ fl oz) water

TOPPING
1 tablespoon sun-dried tomato paste
2 large, mild red or green chillies, halved and deseeded
3 tablespoons chopped mixed herbs, such as parsley, oregano, rosemary and chives
50 g (2 oz) sun-dried tomatoes in oil, drained and sliced
2 plum tomatoes, quartered
150 g (5 oz) baby artichokes in oil, drained
150 g (5 oz) mozzarella cheese, sliced
50 g (2 oz) black olives
salt and pepper

Preparation time:
5 minutes

Cooking time:
10 minutes

Serves: **4**

Oven temperature:
200°C (400°F) Gas Mark 6

5 tablespoons passata (sieved tomatoes)
1 tablespoon red pesto
pinch of salt
4 x 25 cm (10 inch) ready-made pizza dough bases
250 g (8 oz) taleggio cheese, derinded and sliced
175 g (6 oz) fine asparagus spears, trimmed
2 tablespoons olive oil
pepper

Mix together the passata, pesto and salt in a small bowl and spread the mixture over the pizza dough bases. Top with the taleggio and asparagus spears and drizzle with the oil.

Bake the pizzas directly on the shelves at the top of a preheated oven, 200°C (400°F), Gas Mark 6, for 10 minutes or until the asparagus is tender and the pizza bases crisp. Grind over some pepper over the tops before serving.

Put the flour, oil, salt and sun-dried tomato paste in a large bowl. Add the measured water and mix to a soft dough, adding a little more water if necessary.

Roll out the dough on a lightly floured surface to a 28 cm (11 inch) round. Put the round on a large, oiled baking sheet and bake in a preheated oven, 230°C (450°F), Gas Mark 8, for 5 minutes.

Spread the pizza base to within 1 cm (½ inch) of the edge with the sun-dried tomato paste. Cut the chillies in half lengthways again and scatter over the pizza with half the herbs, the tomatoes, artichokes, mozzarella and olives. Scatter the remaining herbs on top and season lightly with salt and pepper. Bake for a further 10–15 minutes until the cheese has melted and the vegetables are beginning to colour.

COOK'S NOTES Look out for fine asparagus spears that will roast quickly. If you can only find large spears, halve them lengthways before scattering over the pizza.

95 Flatbread pizzas with blue cheese

96 Fresh vegetable pizza

Preparation time:
5 minutes

Cooking time:
7–8 minutes

Serves: 4

Oven temperature:
200°C (400°F) Gas Mark 6

4 x 20 cm (8 inch) Mediterranean
  flatbreads
200 g (7 oz) Gorgonzola or dolcelatte
  cheese, crumbled
8 slices of prosciutto
50 g (2 oz) rocket leaves
extra virgin olive oil, for drizzling
pepper

Preparation time:
15 minutes

Cooking time:
10 minutes

Serves: 4

Oven temperature:
230°C (450°F) Gas Mark 8

4 x 25 cm (10 inch) ready-made pizza
  dough bases
5 tablespoons olive oil
2 garlic cloves, crushed
1 red onion, thinly sliced
2 courgettes, thinly sliced lengthways
1 red pepper, cored, deseeded and cut
  into thin strips
1 yellow pepper, cored, deseeded and
  cut into thin strips
4 plum tomatoes, skinned, cored and cut
  into small wedges
500 g (1 lb) fine asparagus tips
4 thyme sprigs, leaves stripped
handful of basil leaves, roughly torn
salt and pepper
75 g (3 oz) Parmesan cheese, freshly
  shaved (optional), to serve

Put the flatbreads on 2 baking sheets and scatter the centres with the blue cheese.

Bake the flatbreads in a preheated oven, 200°C (400°F), Gas Mark 6, for 7–8 minutes until the bases are crisp and the cheese has melted.

Top the pizzas with the prosciutto and rocket leaves, grind over some pepper and drizzle with oil. Serve immediately.

Put the pizza dough bases on to warmed baking sheets, brush with a little of the oil, then arrange the vegetables on the bases. Sprinkle with the thyme and basil.

Season the pizzas well with salt and pepper, drizzle with the remaining oil and bake at the top of a preheated oven, 230°C (450°F), Gas Mark 8, for 10 minutes. The vegetables should be slightly charred around the edges as this adds to the flavour.

Serve immediately, with Parmesan shavings, if you like.

COOK'S NOTES Flatbread is very versatile and, as well making the perfect speedy pizza, it can be used for sandwiches and for dipping. You'll find it in delicatessens, specialist Mediterranean grocers and in some supermarkets.

97 Flatbread pizzas with goats' cheese

98 Warm pasta salad

Preparation time:
10 minutes

Cooking time:
7–8 minutes

Serves: **4**

Oven temperature:
200°C (400°F) Gas Mark 6

4 x 20 cm (8 inch) Mediterranean flatbreads
2 tablespoons sun-dried tomato paste
300 g (10 oz) mozzarella cheese, sliced
6 plum tomatoes, roughly chopped
4 tablespoons olive oil
1 garlic clove, crushed
small handful of basil leaves, roughly torn
100 g (3½ oz) goats' cheese
salt and pepper

Preparation time:
10 minutes, plus standing

Cooking time:
about 10 minutes

Serves: **4**

250 g (8 oz) dried malloreddus or orzo pasta
250 g (8 oz) frozen peas, defrosted
6 tablespoons extra virgin olive oil
6 spring onions, roughly chopped
2 garlic cloves, crushed
8 bottled marinated artichoke hearts, drained and thickly sliced
4 tablespoons chopped mint
2 tablespoons lemon juice
salt and pepper
lemon rind, to garnish

Put the flatbreads on 2 baking sheets and spread with the sun-dried tomato paste. Top with the mozzarella and bake in a preheated oven, 200°C (400°F), Gas Mark 6, for 7–8 minutes until the bases are crisp and the cheese has melted.

Meanwhile, put the tomatoes in a bowl, add the oil, garlic and basil and season well with salt and pepper. Toss well to mix. Top the cooked pizza bases with the tomato mixture and crumble over the goats' cheese. Serve immediately.

Bring a large saucepan of lightly salted water to the boil. Add the pasta, return to the boil and cook for 6 minutes. Add the peas and cook for a further 2–3 minutes until the peas and pasta are tender. Drain well.

Meanwhile, heat 2 tablespoons of the oil in a frying pan, add the spring onions and garlic and cook for 1–2 minutes until softened. Stir in the pasta and peas with the artichokes, mint and the remaining oil.

Toss the ingredients gently until combined, season to taste with salt and pepper, then leave to stand for 10 minutes. Stir in the lemon juice and serve the salad warm, garnished with lemon rind.

COOK'S NOTES Mediterranean flatbreads crisp up beautifully in the oven or under the grill, making them a perfect, time-saving alternative to the classic bread dough pizza base.

COOK'S NOTES Malloreddus is a rice-shaped pasta, traditionally flavoured with saffron, and is available from larger supermarkets and specialist Italian food stores. It is often added to soups.

99 Angel hair pasta with prawns

Preparation time: **5 minutes**	**375 g (12 oz) dried angel hair pasta**
	25 g (1 oz) butter
	4 plum tomatoes, chopped
Cooking time: **8 minutes**	**2 tablespoons brandy**
	200 g (7 oz) cooked peeled prawns, defrosted if frozen
Serves: **4**	**3 tablespoons double cream**
	1 tablespoon chopped tarragon
	salt and pepper

Bring a large saucepan of lightly salted water to the boil. Add the pasta, return to the boil and cook for 5 minutes, or according to the packet instructions, until tender but still firm to the bite. Drain well.

Meanwhile, heat the butter in a frying pan, add the tomatoes and cook for 2–3 minutes until softened. Pour in the brandy, increase the heat to high and cook for 2 minutes.

Add the prawns, cream and tarragon and heat through. Season well with salt and pepper.

Toss the sauce with the hot pasta and serve immediately.

COOK'S NOTES Small prawns, often sweeter than tiger prawns, are ideal for this dish, and convenient frozen ones, defrosted, are fine to use. Make sure you boil off the brandy properly to remove its slightly 'raw' taste before adding the prawns and herbs.

100 Black pasta with monkfish and spinach

Preparation time: **10 minutes**	**375 g (12 oz) dried black (squid ink) pasta**
	25 g (1 oz) butter
	200 g (7 oz) monkfish tail, cut into 2.5 cm (1 inch) cubes
Cooking time: **about 15 minutes**	**2 large red chillies, deseeded and finely chopped**
Serves: **4**	**2 garlic cloves, chopped**
	2 tablespoons Thai fish sauce
Oven temperature: **200°C (400°F) Gas Mark 6**	**150 g (5 oz) baby spinach leaves**
	juice of 2 limes or to taste
	salt
	lime wedges, to serve

Bring a large saucepan of lightly salted water to the boil. Add the pasta, return to the boil and cook for 8–12 minutes, or according to the packet instructions, until tender but still firm to the bite. Drain well, add the butter and toss well to coat evenly.

Meanwhile, cut out a large rectangle of foil. Put the monkfish cubes in the centre and pull the edges of the foil up around the fish. Top the fish with the chillies, garlic and fish sauce. Bring the edges of the foil up to meet and fold over tightly to seal the parcel. Transfer to a baking sheet and cook in a preheated oven, 200°C (400°F), Gas Mark 6, for 8–10 minutes until cooked through.

Carefully open the parcel and toss the contents with the hot pasta. Add the spinach and stir until it has wilted. Add lime juice and salt to taste and serve immediately with lime wedges.

COOK'S NOTES Black pasta, coloured and flavoured with squid ink, has a very subtle taste of fish and looks stunning, making it the perfect choice when entertaining friends or family.

101 Spaghetti with asparagus

Preparation time:	375 g (12 oz) dried spaghetti
10 minutes	375 g (12 oz) asparagus spears, trimmed
	and cut into 8 cm (3 inch) lengths
Cooking time:	5 tablespoons olive oil
10 minutes	50 g (2 oz) butter
	½ teaspoon crushed dried red chilli
Serves: **4**	flakes
	2 garlic cloves, sliced
Oven temperature:	50 g (2 oz) anchovy fillets in oil, drained
200°C (400°F) Gas Mark 6	and chopped
	2 tablespoons lemon juice
	75 g (3 oz) Parmesan cheese, freshly
	shaved
	salt

Bring a large saucepan of lightly salted water to the boil. Add the pasta, return to the boil and cook for 9 minutes, or according to the packet instructions, until tender but still firm to the bite. Drain well.

Meanwhile, arrange the asparagus spears in a roasting tin, drizzle with the oil and dot with the butter. Scatter with the chilli flakes, garlic and anchovies and roast in a preheated oven, 200°C (400°F), Gas Mark 6, for 8 minutes until tender.

Toss the asparagus with the hot pasta and sprinkle over the lemon juice. Scatter the Parmesan shavings over the top, season to taste with salt and serve immediately.

COOK'S NOTES Make this simple, flavoursome dish when asparagus is in season and at its best. You can use other types of long pasta if you prefer, such as linguine or bucatini.

102 Ravioli with burnt sage butter

Preparation time:	500 g (1 lb) good quality fresh ravioli
5 minutes	50 g (2 oz) butter
	50 g (2 oz) pine nuts
Cooking time:	15 sage leaves, sliced
about 10 minutes	2 tablespoons lemon juice
	salt
Serves: **4**	fresh Parmesan cheese shavings,
	to serve

Bring a large saucepan of lightly salted water to the boil. Add the pasta, return to the boil and cook for 6–8 minutes, or according to the packet instructions, until tender but still firm to the bite. Drain well and divide among 4 warmed plates.

Meanwhile, heat the butter in a frying pan, add the pine nuts and sage and cook, stirring, until the pine nuts are lightly browned and the butter is pale golden. Have the lemon juice to hand and, once the butter is the right colour, turn off the heat and quickly pour in the lemon juice.

Season the butter to taste with salt and pour over the hot ravioli. Scatter with Parmesan shavings and serve immediately.

COOK'S NOTES Burnt butter tastes fantastic and is one of the simplest things to make, but the timing is absolutely crucial. You need only to brown the butter a little, so once you see it turning, throw in the lemon juice to prevent it from cooking any further.

103 Roasted tomato and ricotta pasta

104 Pasta with aubergines and pine nuts

Preparation time:	500 g (1 lb) cherry tomatoes, halved
10 minutes	4 tablespoons extra virgin olive oil
	2 teaspoons chopped thyme
Cooking time:	4 garlic cloves, sliced
15–20 minutes	pinch of dried red chilli flakes
	400 g (13 oz) dried pasta
Serves: 4	1 bunch of basil leaves, torn
	125 g (4 oz) ricotta cheese, crumbled
Oven temperature:	salt and pepper
200°C (400°F) Gas Mark 6	

Preparation time:	125 ml (4 fl oz) olive oil
10 minutes	2 aubergines, diced
	2 red onions, sliced
Cooking time:	75 g (3 oz) pine nuts
15 minutes	3 garlic cloves, crushed
	5 tablespoons sun-dried tomato paste
Serves: 4	150 ml (¼ pint) vegetable stock
	300 g (10 oz) cracked pepper-, tomato- or
	mushroom-flavoured fresh ribbon pasta
	100 g (3½ oz) pitted black olives
	salt and pepper
	3 tablespoons roughly chopped flat leaf
	parsley, to garnish

Put the tomatoes in a roasting tin with the oil, thyme, garlic and chilli flakes and season to taste with salt and pepper. Roast in a preheated oven, 200°C (400°F), Gas Mark 6, for 15–20 minutes until the tomatoes have softened and released their juices.

Meanwhile, bring a large saucepan of lightly salted water to the boil. Add the pasta, return to the boil and cook for 8–12 minutes, or according to the packet instructions, until tender but still firm to the bite. Drain the pasta and return it to the pan.

Stir the tomatoes with their pan juices and most of the basil leaves into the pasta and toss gently until combined. Season to taste with salt and pepper and spoon into warmed bowls. Chop the remaining basil, mix into the ricotta and season to taste with salt and pepper. Spoon into a serving dish for people to spoon on to the pasta.

Heat the oil in a large frying pan, add the aubergines and onions and cook for 8–10 minutes until golden and tender. Add the pine nuts and garlic and cook for 2 minutes. Stir in the sun-dried tomato paste and stock and cook for 2 minutes.

Meanwhile, bring a large saucepan of lightly salted water to the boil. Add the pasta, return to the boil and cook for 2 minutes, or according to the packet instructions, until tender but still firm to the bite.

Drain the pasta and return to the pan. Add the sauce and olives, season to taste with salt and pepper and toss together over a medium heat for 1 minute until combined. Serve garnished with the parsley.

COOK'S NOTES This piquant, herb-scented dish can be made with just about any shape or variety of pasta you like. Always check the packet instructions because cooking times will vary.

105 Pasta with radicchio and cheese crumbs

Preparation time:
5 minutes

Cooking time:
15 minutes

Serves: **2**

175 g (6 oz) dried spaghetti
65 g (2½ oz) butter
25 g (1 oz) fresh white breadcrumbs
15 g (½ oz) Parmesan cheese, freshly grated
2 shallots, finely chopped
1 garlic clove, sliced
1 head of radicchio, shredded
dash of lemon juice
salt and pepper

Bring a large saucepan of lightly salted water to the boil. Add the pasta, return to the boil and cook for 9 minutes, or according to the packet instructions, until tender but still firm to the bite. Drain well, reserving 2 tablespoons of the cooking water.

Meanwhile, heat half the butter in a frying pan, add the breadcrumbs and cook for 5 minutes or until evenly golden and crisp. Transfer to a bowl, leave to cool slightly, then stir in the Parmesan.

Heat the remaining butter in a wok or large saucepan, add the shallots and garlic and cook for 5 minutes until softened. Add the radicchio and lemon juice and season to taste with salt and pepper. Cook over a low heat, stirring, for 2 minutes until the radicchio has wilted. Add the pasta, toss until heated through and serve topped with the cheese crumbs.

106 Pasta with spinach and goats' cheese

Preparation time:
10 minutes

Cooking time:
8 minutes

Serves: **4**

500 g (1 lb) baby spinach leaves
pinch of grated nutmeg, plus extra to serve
125 g (4 oz) goats' cheese, roughly chopped
150 ml (¼ pint) low-fat crème fraîche
2 teaspoons Dijon mustard
500 g (1 lb) fresh wholewheat pasta
75 g (3 oz) pine kernels, toasted
1 tablespoon chopped parsley
2 tablespoons grated Parmesan cheese
salt and pepper

Blanch the spinach leaves in boiling water for 1 minute. Drain the leaves, squeezing out any excess water, and roughly chop. Mix the spinach with the grated nutmeg, goats' cheese, crème fraîche and mustard.

Bring a pan of water to the boil, add the pasta, return to the boil and cook for 4–5 minutes, or according to the packet instructions, until tender. Drain well.

Return the hot pasta immediately to the pan and add the spinach mixture, salt, pepper and pine kernels and toss together. Add the parsley and Parmesan and a touch more grated nutmeg and serve while still piping hot.

107 Pasta salad with crab

Preparation time:
5 minutes, plus cooling

Cooking time:
10 minutes

Serves: **1**

150 g (5 oz) dried rigatoni or other pasta shape
finely grated rind and juice of ½ lime
2 tablespoons crème fraîche
85 g (3½ oz) can crabmeat, drained
8 cherry tomatoes, halved
handful of rocket leaves

Bring a large saucepan of lightly salted water to the boil. Add the pasta, return to the boil and cook for 8–10 minutes, or according to the packet instructions, until tender but still firm to the bite. Drain well and leave to cool for 15 minutes.

Meanwhile, mix together the lime rind and juice, crème fraîche and crabmeat in a large bowl.

Add the cooled pasta to the sauce mixture and mix again. Add the tomatoes and rocket leaves, toss together and serve.

108 Lemon and basil orzo

Preparation time:
10 minutes

Cooking time:
10 minutes

Serves: **4**

2 garlic cloves, crushed
large handful of basil leaves
5 tablespoons olive oil
finely grated rind and juice of 2 lemons
150 g (5 oz) Parmesan cheese, freshly grated
300 g (10 oz) dried orzo
salt and pepper

Put the garlic, basil, oil and lemon rind and juice in a food processor and process until smooth, then add the Parmesan, process again briefly and season to taste with salt and pepper. Alternatively, pound the garlic, basil, oil and lemon rind and juice in a mortar with a pestle, then add the Parmesan, blend well and season to taste with salt and pepper.

Meanwhile, bring a large saucepan of lightly salted water to the boil. Add the pasta, return to the boil and cook for 6–8 minutes, or according to the packet instructions, until tender but still firm to the bite.

Drain the pasta well and return to the pan. Add the basil mixture and toss well to coat evenly. Serve immediately.

COOK'S NOTES Orzo pasta is small and shaped like large grains of rice. This recipe uses flavoursome and simple ingredients – make sure you buy good quality Parmesan as this really makes the dish special.

109 Lemon and chilli prawn linguine

Preparation time:
15 minutes

Cooking time:
10 minutes

Serves: **4**

375 g (12 oz) dried linguine or spaghetti
1 tablespoon olive oil
1 tablespoon butter
1 garlic clove, finely chopped
2 spring onions, thinly sliced
2 red chillies, deseeded and thinly sliced
425 g (14 oz) raw tiger prawns, peeled and deveined but tails left intact
2 tablespoons lemon juice
2 tablespoons finely chopped fresh coriander leaves, plus extra whole leaves to garnish
salt and pepper

Bring a large saucepan of lightly salted water to the boil. Add the pasta, return to the boil and cook for 9 minutes, or according to the packet instructions, until tender but still firm to the bite. Drain well.

Meanwhile, heat the oil and butter in a large frying pan, add the garlic, spring onions and chillies and cook for 2–3 minutes. Add the prawns and cook for 3–4 minutes or until they turn pink and are just cooked through.

Stir in the lemon juice and coriander, then remove from the heat. Add the pasta, season well with salt and pepper and toss together. Serve immediately, garnished with coriander leaves.

110 Tuna lasagne with rocket

Preparation time:
10 minutes

Cooking time:
5–10 minutes

Serves: **4**

8 sheets of fresh lasagne
1 teaspoon olive oil
1 bunch of spring onions, sliced
2 courgettes, diced
500 g (1 lb) cherry tomatoes, quartered
2 x 200 g (7 oz) cans tuna in spring water, drained
65 g (2½ oz) rocket leaves
4 teaspoons pesto
pepper
basil leaves, to garnish

Bring a large saucepan of salted water to the boil. Add the lasagne, a few sheets at a time, checking that it does not stick together, return to the boil and cook for 3 minutes, or according to the packet instructions, until tender but still firm to the bite. Drain and return to the pan to keep warm.

Meanwhile, heat the oil in a frying pan, add the spring onions and courgettes and cook for 3 minutes. Remove from the heat, add the tomatoes, tuna and rocket leaves and gently toss together.

Put a little of the tuna mixture on 4 serving plates and top with a sheet of the cooked lasagne. Spoon the remaining tuna mixture over the lasagne, then top with the remaining sheets of lasagne. Season well with pepper, top with a spoonful of pesto and garnish with basil leaves. Serve immediately.

COOK'S NOTES This is a quick version of the classic lasagne. It doesn't require oven cooking so it can be ready in a fraction of the time. Have fun with the presentation and serve as a quick dinner party dish.

111 Mushroom and mozzarella stacks

Preparation time:
10 minutes

Cooking time:
20 minutes

Serves: 4

2 tablespoons olive oil, plus extra for oiling
50 g (2 oz) butter
2 onions, chopped
2 garlic cloves, crushed
500 g (1 lb) mushrooms, sliced
4 tablespoons double cream
4 tablespoons dry white wine
1 teaspoon chopped thyme
8 sheets of fresh lasagne
2 canned pimientos, drained and thickly sliced
125 g (4 oz) baby spinach leaves, chopped
125 g (4 oz) packet of buffalo mozzarella cheese, drained and sliced
50 g (2 oz) Parmesan cheese, freshly shaved
salt and pepper

Heat the oil and butter in a saucepan, add the onions and cook over a medium heat for 3 minutes. Add the garlic and cook, stirring, for 1 minute. Add the mushrooms, increase the heat and cook for 5 minutes. Add the cream, wine and thyme, season to taste with salt and pepper and simmer for 4 minutes.

Meanwhile, bring a large saucepan of lightly salted water to the boil. Add the lasagne, a few sheets at a time, checking that it does not stick together, return to the boil and cook for 3 minutes, or according to the packet instructions, until tender but still firm to the bite. Drain and transfer 4 pieces to a well-oiled, large ovenproof dish.

Put a generous spoonful of mushroom mixture on each piece of lasagne in the dish, add some pimiento slices and half the spinach and top with another piece of lasagne. Add the remaining spinach, the mozzarella and top with the remaining mushroom mixture. Finish with some Parmesan shavings. Put the lasagne stacks under a very hot preheated grill and cook for 5 minutes or until the mushroom mixture is bubbling and the Parmesan is golden.

112 Pasta bake with spinach and ham

Preparation time:
10 minutes

Cooking time:
20 minutes

Serves: 4

Oven temperature:
200°C (400°F) Gas Mark 6

2 tablespoons olive oil, plus extra for oiling
1 onion, chopped
1 garlic clove, crushed
750 g (1½ lb) baby spinach leaves, chopped
pinch of freshly grated nutmeg
8 sheets of no-precook lasagne
250 g (8 oz) ham, chopped into large chunks
125 g (4 oz) packet of buffalo mozzarella cheese, drained and thinly sliced
125 g (4 oz) fontina cheese, grated
salt and pepper

Heat the oil in a saucepan, add the onion and garlic and cook for 3 minutes. Add the spinach and mix well. Cook for 2 minutes until the spinach starts to wilt. Add the nutmeg and season to taste with salt and pepper.

Put a layer of lasagne in the base of a lightly oiled, large, shallow baking dish, followed by a layer of the spinach mixture, a layer of ham, then a layer of mozzarella. Repeat until all the ingredients are used up, finishing with a layer of lasagne and the fontina.

Bake the pasta at the top of a preheated oven, 200°C (400°F), Gas Mark 6, for 15 minutes until golden brown and bubbling.

COOK'S NOTES Buffalo mozzarella has the richest flavour and creamiest texture so it's important to buy this variety. It will melt and combine with the other ingredients, while the fontina will create a lovely golden topping.

113 Courgettes with linguine and gremolata

Preparation time:
10 minutes

Cooking time:
12 minutes

Serves: **4**

450 g (14½ oz) dried linguine
2 tablespoons olive oil
6 large courgettes, thickly sliced
8 spring onions, thinly sliced
fresh Parmesan cheese shavings,
** to serve**

GREMOLATA
finely grated rind of 2 lemons
1 tablespoon oil
10 tablespoons chopped flat leaf parsley
2 garlic cloves, crushed

Bring a large saucepan of lightly salted water to the boil. Add the pasta, return to the boil and cook for 9 minutes, or according to the packet instructions, until tender but still firm to the bite.

Meanwhile, heat the oil in a nonstick frying pan, add the courgettes and cook over a high heat for 10 minutes or until browned. Add the spring onions and cook for 1–2 minutes.

To make the gremolata, mix together all the ingredients in a bowl.

Drain the pasta well and return to the pan. Stir in the courgette mixture and gremolata. Serve immediately, topped with Parmesan shavings.

COOK'S NOTES Prepare the gremola in advance to make this pasta dish even quicker. Linguine is similar to spaghetti but the strands are thinner so it has a more delicate texture.

114 Risotto with wild mushrooms and sage

Preparation time:
10 minutes

Cooking time:
20 minutes

Serves: **4**

1 litre (1¾ pints) vegetable stock
125 g (4 oz) butter
1 tablespoon olive oil
1 garlic clove, crushed
1 onion, finely diced
250 g (8 oz) wild mushrooms, such as
** morels, porcini, chanterelles or**
** cultivated open cap mushrooms,**
** halved or quartered**
300 g (10 oz) risotto rice
75 ml (3 fl oz) dry white wine
1 tablespoon chopped sage
salt and pepper
125 g (4 oz) Parmesan cheese, freshly
** grated, to serve**
truffle oil, to drizzle (optional)

Pour the stock into a saucepan and bring to a gentle simmer.

Heat half the butter and all the oil in a heavy-based saucepan, add the garlic and onion and cook gently for 3 minutes. Add the mushrooms and cook gently for 2 minutes. Add the rice and cook, stirring, for 1 minute. Add enough stock to just cover the rice and stir well. Simmer gently, stirring frequently.

When most of the liquid has been absorbed, add more stock. Continue adding the stock in stages and stirring until it has all been absorbed. Add the wine with the final amount of stock, mix well and cook for 2 minutes.

Remove te risotto from the heat and add the remaining butter, sage and salt and pepper to taste. Mix well and serve immediately with Parmesan, drizzled with truffle oil, if you like.

115 Green risotto

116 Asparagus and dolcelatte risotto

Preparation time:
10 minutes

Cooking time:
20 minutes

Serves: **4**

1 litre (1¾ pints) vegetable stock
125 g (4 oz) butter
1 tablespoon olive oil
1 garlic clove, crushed
1 onion, finely diced
300 g (10 oz) risotto rice
125 g (4 oz) green beans, trimmed and cut
  into short lengths
125 g (4 oz) frozen peas
125 g (4 oz) frozen broad beans
125 g (4 oz) asparagus tips
125 g (4 oz) baby spinach leaves,
  chopped
75 ml (3 fl oz) dry vermouth or white wine
2 tablespoons chopped parsley
125 g (4 oz) Parmesan cheese, freshly
  grated
salt and pepper

Preparation time:
5 minutes

Cooking time:
25 minutes

Serves: **4**

1.2 litres (2 pints) vegetable stock
1 teaspoon olive oil
1 small onion, finely chopped
300 g (10 oz) asparagus spears, halved
  and the stem ends finely sliced
375 g (12 oz) risotto rice
2 tablespoons dry white wine
75 g (3 oz) dolcelatte cheese, chopped
2 tablespoons chopped parsley
rocket and tomato salad, to serve

Pour the stock into a saucepan and bring to a gentle simmer.

Heat the oil in a large, nonstick frying pan, add the onion and sliced asparagus and cook for 2–3 minutes until beginning to soften. Add the rice and cook, stirring, for 1 minute, then add the wine and cook until it has been absorbed. Add enough stock to just cover the rice and stir well. Simmer gently, stirring frequently.

When most of the liquid has been absorbed, add more stock. Continue adding the stock in stages and stirring until it has all been absorbed. Add the asparagus tips with the final amount of stock and mix well.

Remove the risotto from the heat and gently stir through the dolcelatte and parsley. Serve immediately with a rocket and tomato salad.

Pour the stock into a saucepan and bring to a gentle simmer.

Heat half the butter and the oil in a heavy-based saucepan, add the garlic and onion and cook gently for 5 minutes. Add the rice and cook, stirring, for 1 minute. Add enough stock to just cover the rice and stir well. Simmer gently, stirring frequently.

When most of the liquid has been absorbed, add more stock and stir well. Continue adding the stock in stages and stirring until it has all been absorbed. Add the vegetables and vermouth or wine with the final amount of stock, mix well and cook for 2 minutes.

Remove the risotto from the heat and add the remaining butter, the parsley, Parmesan and salt and pepper to taste. Mix well and serve immediately.

COOK'S NOTES You need to use special risotto rice such as carnoroli or arborio, as the grains are short and plump and can soak up a lot of liquid.

117 Nasi goreng

Preparation time:	2 tablespoons vegetable oil
10 minutes	150 g (5 oz) boneless, skinless chicken
	breast, finely chopped
Cooking time:	50 g (2 oz) cooked peeled prawns,
10 minutes	defrosted if frozen
	1 garlic clove, crushed
Serves: **4**	1 carrot, grated
	¼ white cabbage, thinly sliced
	1 egg, beaten
	300 g (10 oz) cold cooked basmati rice
	2 tablespoons ketchup manis (sweet soy
	sauce)
	½ teaspoon sesame oil
	1 tablespoon chilli sauce
	1 red chilli, deseeded and cut into strips,
	to garnish

Heat the oil in a wok or large frying pan, add the chicken and stir-fry for 1 minute. Add the prawns, garlic, carrot and cabbage and stir-fry for 3–4 minutes.

Pour in the egg and spread it out using a wooden spoon. Cook until set, then add the rice and break up the egg, stirring it in.

Add the ketchup manis, sesame oil and chilli sauce and heat through. Serve immediately, garnished with the chilli strips.

118 Chicken, pea and mint risotto

Preparation time:	25 g (1 oz) butter
5 minutes	1 onion, finely chopped
	150 g (5 oz) boneless, skinless chicken
Cooking time:	breast, cut into strips
25 minutes	200 g (7 oz) risotto rice
	1 teaspoon fennel seeds
Serves: **4**	900 ml (1½ pints) hot chicken stock
	75 g (3 oz) frozen peas, defrosted
Oven temperature:	finely grated rind and juice of 1 lemon
200°C (400°F) Gas Mark 6	2 tablespoons double cream
	100 g (3½ oz) Parmesan cheese, freshly
	grated
	2 tablespoons chopped mint
	salt and pepper

Heat the butter in a flameproof casserole, add the onion and chicken and cook for 3 minutes. Add the rice and fennel seeds and cook, stirring, for 30 seconds, then add the stock and peas.

Cover the casserole tightly and cook in a preheated oven, 200°C (400°F), Gas Mark 6, for 20 minutes until the rice is tender and all the liquid has been absorbed.

Stir in the lemon rind and juice, cream and Parmesan and season to taste with salt and pepper. Cover and leave to stand for 2 minutes, then stir in the mint. Serve immediately.

COOK'S NOTES Risotto cooked in the oven is incredibly simple. The final result is not usually as creamy as a risotto stirred over the hob, but this recipe includes a little cream to add at the end to make up for it. Be sure to use arborio or another risotto rice because you cannot achieve the taste and texture of an authentic risotto using any other rice.

119 Jambalaya

Preparation time:
10 minutes

Cooking time:
15 minutes

Serves: 4

2 tablespoons olive oil
1 onion, finely chopped
100 g (3½ oz) frankfurters or smoked
   sausages, sliced
100 g (3½ oz) cooked chicken, cubed
125 g (4 oz) quick-cooking rice
400 g (13 oz) can chopped tomatoes
200 g (7 oz) bottled roasted peppers in oil,
   drained and chopped
600 ml (1 pint) chicken stock
2 bay leaves
pinch of ground allspice
salt and pepper
chopped oregano, to garnish
soured cream, to serve (optional)

Heat the oil in a large frying pan, add the onion and cook for 3 minutes. Add the sausages and chicken and cook for 2 minutes.

Add the rice, tomatoes, peppers, stock, bay leaves and allspice. Cover the pan and simmer very gently for 10 minutes or until the rice is tender and all the liquid has been absorbed.

Season to taste with salt and pepper and scatter with oregano. Serve with soured cream, if you like.

COOK'S NOTES This Creole dish is a great way of making a quick, delicious meal from the leftovers of a roast chicken. Oregano, which is sprinkled over just before serving, is one of the few herbs that retains its flavour when dried, so if you can't find the fresh herb, use a little of the dried version instead.

120 Beetroot risotto with blue cheese

Preparation time:
5 minutes

Cooking time:
25 minutes

Serves: 4

Oven temperature:
200°C (400°F) Gas Mark 6

3 tablespoons olive oil
1 red onion, finely chopped
250 g (8 oz) cooked beetroot in natural
   juices, chopped
200 g (7 oz) risotto rice
600 ml (1 pint) vegetable stock
150 ml (¼ pint) fruity red wine, such as
   Merlot
150 g (5 oz) dolcelatte or other blue
   cheese, crumbled
salt and pepper

TO SERVE
50 g (2 oz) rocket leaves
25 g (1 oz) pecan nuts, chopped and
   toasted

Heat the oil in a flameproof casserole, add the onion and cook for 2 minutes. Add the beetroot and rice and cook, stirring, for 1 minute, then pour in the stock and wine.

Cover the casserole tightly and cook in a preheated oven, 200°C (400°F), Gas Mark 6, for 20 minutes until the rice is tender and all the liquid has been absorbed. Stir in the blue cheese and season to taste with salt and pepper. Divide the risotto among 4 warmed serving bowls, scatter with the rocket leaves and pecan nuts and serve immediately.

COOK'S NOTES Vacuum-packed beetroot is best for this dish – it is quick, convenient and gives a wonderful jewel-like colour to the risotto. However, be sure to choose beetroot in natural juice, not vinegar, otherwise the flavour of the dish will be spoilt.

121 Noodle pancakes with stir-fried vegetables

122 Vegetable noodles in coconut milk

Preparation time:
15 minutes

Cooking time:
10 minutes

Serves: **4**

175 g (6 oz) dried wide rice noodles
1 green chilli, deseeded and sliced
2.5 cm (1 inch) piece of fresh root ginger,
  peeled and grated
3 tablespoons chopped fresh coriander
2 teaspoons plain flour
2 teaspoons groundnut oil, plus extra for
  shallow-frying

STIR-FRIED VEGETABLES
125 g (4 oz) broccoli
2 tablespoons groundnut oil
1 small onion, sliced
1 red pepper, cored, deseeded and sliced
1 yellow or orange pepper, cored,
  deseeded and sliced
125 g (4 oz) sugar snap peas
6 tablespoons hoisin sauce
1 tablespoon lime juice
salt and pepper

Preparation time:
10 minutes

Cooking time:
12 minutes

Serves: **4**

125 g (4 oz) dried medium egg noodles
2 tablespoons groundnut or vegetable oil
1 onion, chopped
1 red bird's eye chilli, deseeded and
  sliced
3 garlic cloves, sliced
5 cm (2 inch) piece of fresh root ginger,
  peeled and grated
2 teaspoons ground coriander
½ teaspoon ground turmeric
1 lemon grass stalk, thinly sliced
400 ml (14 fl oz) can coconut milk
300 ml (½ pint) vegetable stock
125 g (4 oz) spring greens or cabbage,
  finely shredded
275 g (9 oz) runner beans or green beans,
  trimmed and diagonally sliced
150 g (5 oz) shiitake mushrooms, sliced
75 g (3 oz) unsalted peanuts
salt and pepper

Bring a large saucepan of lightly salted water to the boil. Add the noodles, return to the boil and cook for 3 minutes. Drain well. Transfer to a bowl, add the chilli, ginger, coriander, flour and 2 teaspoons oil and mix well.

Meanwhile, thinly slice the broccoli stalks and cut the florets into small pieces. Blanch the stalks in boiling water for 30 seconds, add the florets and blanch for 30 seconds. Drain well.

Heat 1 cm (½ inch) oil in a frying pan. Add 4 large separate spoonfuls of the noodles (half the mixture) and shallow-fry for 5 minutes until crisp. Drain on kitchen paper. Keep warm while cooking the remainder.

Meanwhile, heat the 2 tablespoons oil in a wok or large frying pan, add the onion and stir-fry for 2 minutes. Add the peppers and stir-fry for 3 minutes. Add the broccoli, sugar snap peas, hoisin sauce, lime juice and salt and pepper to taste and heat through. To serve, put 2 pancakes on each of 4 serving plates and pile the vegetables on top.

Soak the noodles in a saucepan of boiling water for 4 minutes, or according to the packet instructions, until just tender.

Meanwhile, heat the oil in a large saucepan, add the onion, chilli, garlic, ginger, coriander, turmeric and lemon grass and cook gently for 5 minutes.

Drain the noodles. Add the coconut milk and stock to the onion mixture and bring just to the boil. Reduce the heat and stir in the spring greens or cabbage, beans, mushrooms and drained noodles. Cover and simmer for 5 minutes. Stir in the peanuts and season to taste with salt and pepper. Serve in deep bowls.

123 Thai fried noodles

Preparation time:
10 minutes, plus soaking

Cooking time:
about 7 minutes

Serves: **4**

250 g (8 oz) flat rice noodles
2 tablespoons vegetable oil
**150 g (5 oz) raw tiger prawns, peeled and
  deveined**
2 garlic cloves, crushed
1 egg, beaten
1 carrot, grated
200 g (7 oz) bean sprouts
1 tablespoon brown sugar
3 tablespoons Thai fish sauce
2 tablespoons lime juice

TO SERVE
50 g (2 oz) unsalted raw peanuts, toasted
1 red chilli, thinly sliced
4 spring onions, sliced
fresh coriander sprigs
lime wedges

Soak the noodles in a saucepan of lightly salted boiling water for 10 minutes, or according to the packet instructions, until just tender. Drain and set aside.

Meanwhile, heat the oil in a wok or large frying pan over a high heat, add the prawns and garlic and stir-fry for 1 minute. Push to one side of the wok and add the egg, stir until lightly scrambled and then add all the remaining ingredients, including the noodles.

Toss thoroughly until all the ingredients are well combined and heated through. Transfer to a large serving dish, top with the peanuts, chilli, spring onions and coriander and serve with lime wedges.

COOK'S NOTES Although there are a lot of ingredients in this recipe it is still very quick to prepare – the key is to have everything to hand before you begin.

124 Stir-fried noodles with mushrooms

Preparation time:
10 minutes

Cooking time:
10 minutes

Serves: **4**

225 g (7½ oz) dried thread egg noodles
1 tablespoon corn oil
1 large onion, sliced lengthways
**1 cm (½ inch) piece of fresh root ginger,
  peeled and finely chopped**
200 g (7 oz) field or portobello mushrooms
125 g (4 oz) bean sprouts
**2 large red peppers, cored, deseeded and
  thinly sliced**
1 tablespoon plum sauce
2 tablespoons light soy sauce
**6 spring onions, diagonally sliced into
  1.5 cm (¾ inch) pieces**

Bring a large saucepan of lightly salted water to the boil. Add the noodles, return to the boil and cook for 3–4 minutes, or according to the packet instructions, until just tender. Drain, rinse under cold running water and drain again.

Meanwhile, heat the oil in a wok or large frying pan over a high heat, add the onion and ginger and stir-fry for 2–3 minutes. Add the mushrooms and stir-fry over a medium heat for 1–2 minutes.

Stir in the bean sprouts, red peppers, plum sauce, soy sauce and spring onions and cook, stirring occasionally, for a further few minutes.

Stir in the noodles, taste and adjust the seasoning, if necessary, and heat through before serving.

COOK'S NOTES Try to resist the temptation to stir the noodles too much while they are cooking, or they will get very tangled.

5 Vegetarian

125 Chilli tofu kebabs

126 Nut koftas with minted yogurt

Preparation time:
10 minutes, plus soaking

Cooking time:
6–8 minutes

Serves: **4**

150 g (5 oz) bulgar wheat
250 g (8 oz) firm tofu
50 g (2 oz) fresh white breadcrumbs
75 g (3 oz) vegetarian bacon, diced (optional)
2 garlic cloves, crushed
25 g (1 oz) fresh root ginger, peeled and grated
½ teaspoon dried red chilli flakes
1 small red onion, finely chopped
10 large mint leaves, chopped
1 egg
2 tablespoons groundnut or soya oil
½ small ripe mango, peeled, stoned and finely chopped
2 teaspoons lime juice
100 ml (3½ fl oz) natural soya yogurt
salt
crisp salad leaves, to serve

Preparation time:
15 minutes

Cooking time:
10 minutes

Serves: **4**

5–6 tablespoons groundnut or vegetable oil
1 onion, chopped
½ teaspoon crushed dried red chilli flakes
2 garlic cloves, roughly chopped
1 tablespoon medium curry paste
400 g (13 oz) can borlotti or cannellini beans, drained and rinsed
125 g (4 oz) ground almonds
75 g (3 oz) honey-roast or salted almonds, chopped
1 small egg
200 ml (7 fl oz) Greek yogurt
2 tablespoons chopped mint
1 tablespoon lemon juice
salt and pepper
mint sprigs, to garnish
warm naan bread, to serve

Put the bulgar wheat in a bowl, cover with plenty of boiling water and leave to soak for 15 minutes, then drain thoroughly. Meanwhile, soak 8 bamboo skewers in cold water until required.

Pat the tofu dry with kitchen paper. Put it in a food processor with the bulgar wheat and process to a thick paste. Tip the mixture into a bowl and add the breadcrumbs, bacon, if using, garlic, ginger, chilli flakes, onion, mint and a little salt. Add the egg and beat the mixture well to form a thick paste.

Divide the mixture into 8 evenly sized balls. Thread a ball on to each skewer and flatten into a sausage shape. Brush with the oil.

Cook the skewers under a preheated medium grill, turning once or twice, for 6–8 minutes until golden. Meanwhile, mix together the mango, lime juice and yogurt in a small serving dish. Serve the kebabs with crisp salad leaves and the mango yogurt.

Heat 3 tablespoons of the oil in a frying pan, add the onion and cook for 4 minutes. Add the chilli flakes, garlic and curry paste and cook, stirring constantly, for 1 minute. Transfer to a food processor with the beans, nuts, egg and salt and pepper to taste and process until the mixture starts to bind together.

Using lightly floured hands, divide the mixture into 8 portions, then mould each around a metal skewer, forming it into a sausage shape about 2.5 cm (1 inch) thick. Put them on a foil-lined grill rack and brush with 1 tablespoon of the remaining oil. Cook under a preheated medium grill, turning once, for 5 minutes or until golden.

Meanwhile, mix together the yogurt and mint in a small serving bowl and season to taste with salt and pepper. Mix the remaining oil, lemon juice and a little salt and pepper in a separate bowl.

Brush the koftas with the lemon dressing and serve with the yogurt dressing on warm naan bread, garnished with mint sprigs.

127 Smoked tofu and apricot sausages

Preparation time:
15 minutes

Cooking time:
10 minutes

Serves: **4**

225 g (7½ oz) smoked tofu
4 tablespoons olive or soya oil
1 large onion, roughly chopped
2 celery sticks, roughly chopped
100 g (3½ oz) ready-to-eat dried apricots,
  roughly chopped
50 g (2 oz) fresh white breadcrumbs
1 egg
1 tablespoon chopped sage
plain flour, for dusting
salt and pepper

Pat the tofu dry on kitchen paper and tear into chunks. Heat the half the oil in a frying pan, add the onion and celery and cook for 5 minutes. Tip the onion and celery into a food processor and add the tofu and apricots. Process the ingredients to a chunky paste.

Tip the mixture into a large bowl and add the breadcrumbs, egg and sage. Season to taste with salt and pepper and beat well until evenly combined.

Divide the mixture into 8 portions. Using lightly floured hands, shape each portion into a sausage, pressing the mixture together firmly. Heat the remaining oil in a nonstick frying pan, add the sausages and cook for 5 minutes or until golden all over.

COOK'S NOTES This quantity makes 8 small sausages, so you might want to make double the quantity for people with larger appetites. Serve with chunky chips and a spicy relish.

128 Tofu burgers with cucumber relish

Preparation time:
15 minutes

Cooking time:
15 minutes

Serves: **4**

4 tablespoons soya or groundnut oil
1 small red onion, finely chopped
1 celery stick, finely chopped
2 garlic cloves, crushed
200 g (7 oz) can red kidney beans,
  drained and rinsed
75 g (3 oz) salted peanuts
250 g (8 oz) firm tofu
2 teaspoons medium curry paste
50 g (2 oz) fresh white breadcrumbs
1 egg
plain flour, for dusting (optional)
½ small cucumber, peeled, deseeded and
  chopped
2 tablespoons chopped flat leaf parsley
1 tablespoon white wine vinegar
2 teaspoons caster sugar
burger buns and lettuce, to serve

Heat 1 tablespoon of the oil in a frying pan, add all but 1 tablespoon of the onion and the celery and cook for 5 minutes. Add the garlic and cook for 2 minutes.

Put the beans in a bowl and mash lightly with a fork. Put the peanuts in a food processor and process until finely chopped. Pat the tofu dry with kitchen paper, break it into pieces and add to the food processor. Process until the tofu is crumbly, then add the mixture to the beans together with the fried vegetables, curry paste, breadcrumbs and egg. Mix well to form a thick paste.

Divide the mixture into 4 portions and shape into burgers, dusting your hands with flour if the mixture is sticky. Heat the remaining oil in the pan, add the burgers and cook for 4 minutes on each side or until golden.

Meanwhile, mix the cucumber with the remaining tablespoon of onion, the parsley, vinegar and sugar in a small bowl. Line the burger buns with lettuce, add the burgers and serve with the relish.

129 Mediterranean goats' cheese omelette

130 Pea and mint frittata

Preparation time:
10 minutes

Cooking time:
15–20 minutes

Serves: **4**

4 tablespoons extra virgin olive oil
500 g (1 lb) cherry tomatoes, halved
a little chopped basil
12 eggs
2 tablespoons wholegrain mustard
50 g (2 oz) butter
100 g (3½ oz) soft goats' cheese, diced
salt and pepper
watercress, to garnish

Heat the oil in a large frying pan, add the tomatoes and cook for 2–3 minutes until softened (you may have to do this in 2 batches). Add the basil and salt and pepper to taste, transfer to a bowl and keep warm.

Beat the eggs with the mustard in a bowl and season to taste with salt and pepper. Melt a quarter of the butter in an omelette pan or small frying pan until it stops foaming, then swirl in a quarter of the egg mixture. Fork over the omelette so that it cooks evenly.

As soon as the omelette is set on the bottom but still a little runny in the centre, scatter over a quarter of the goats' cheese and cook for a further 30 seconds. Carefully slide the omelette on to a warmed serving plate, folding it in half as you go. Keep it warm in a low oven while you repeat with the remaining mixture to make 3 more omelettes. Serve with the tomatoes, garnished with watercress.

Preparation time:
10 minutes

Cooking time:
20 minutes

Serves: **4**

200 g (7 oz) sweet potato, peeled and
thinly sliced
100 g (3½ oz) fresh or frozen peas
1 tablespoon olive oil
2 shallots, thinly sliced
1 red pepper, cored, deseeded and thinly
sliced lengthways
6 eggs, beaten
1 tablespoon milk
1 tablespoon freshly grated Parmesan
cheese
4 tablespoons chopped mint
pepper
frisée, to serve

Bring a large saucepan of water to the boil, add the sweet potato slices and peas and cook for 5 minutes or until the sweet potato is just tender. Drain.

Heat the oil in a deep, nonstick, ovenproof frying pan, add the shallots and red pepper and cook for 1–2 minutes. Add the peas and sweet potato slices and warm through for a further 2 minutes.

Mix together the eggs, milk and Parmesan in a bowl and season to taste with pepper. Pour the egg mixture over the vegetables, lifting the vegetables slightly so that the egg runs to the base of the pan. Cook over a low heat until starting to set and lightly stir in the mint.

Put the pan under a preheated medium-high grill and cook for 3–4 minutes until the top of the frittata is brown and fluffy. Remove the frittata from the pan, cut it into wedges and serve with a grind of pepper, accompanied by some frisée.

COOK'S NOTES Use a combination of red and yellow cherry tomatoes for maximum colour impact.

131 Aubergine cannelloni

Preparation time:
15 minutes

Cooking time:
15 minutes

Serves: 4

**4 aubergines, about 250 g (8 oz) each,
  thinly sliced lengthways**
olive oil, for brushing
250 g (8 oz) ricotta cheese
250 g (8 oz) soft goats' cheese
**150 g (5 oz) Parmesan cheese, grated,
  plus extra shavings to serve**
4 tablespoons chopped basil
**4 large pieces of sun-dried tomato in oil,
  drained and sliced**
rocket leaves, to garnish

TOMATO SAUCE
2 tablespoons olive oil
1 onion, chopped
2 garlic cloves, crushed
**1 kg (2 lb) sun-ripened tomatoes,
  skinned, deseeded and chopped**
150 ml (¼ pint) vegetable stock
1 tablespoon sun-dried tomato purée
salt and pepper

To make the tomato sauce, heat the oil in a saucepan, add the onion and cook gently, until soft. Stir in the garlic, tomatoes, stock and tomato purée, then simmer until thickened to a fairly light sauce. Season to taste.

Meanwhile, brush the aubergine slices lightly with oil. Cook under a preheated grill until evenly browned on both sides. Drain on kitchen paper.

Mix together the ricotta and goats' cheeses, 125 g (4 oz) of the Parmesan and the chopped basil. Season to taste. Spoon the cheese mixture along each aubergine slice and add a sun-dried tomato slice. Roll the aubergine slices, from the short end, around the filling. Place the rolls, seam side down, in a single layer in a shallow, ovenproof dish and sprinkle with the remaining Parmesan. Place under a preheated grill for 5 minutes until the filling is hot.

Serve on warmed plates. Scatter over shavings of Parmesan and garnish with rocket leaves. Serve the tomato sauce separately.

132 Sweet potato and goats' cheese frittata

Preparation time:
10 minutes

Cooking time:
20 minutes

Serves: 4

**500 g (1 lb) sweet potatoes, peeled and
  sliced**
1 teaspoon olive oil
5 spring onions, sliced
2 tablespoons chopped fresh coriander
4 large eggs, beaten
**100 g (3½ oz) round goats' cheese with
  rind, cut into 4 slices**
pepper
crisp green salad, to serve

Bring a large saucepan of boiling water to the boil, add the sweet potato slices and cook for 7–8 minutes until tender. Drain well.

Heat the oil in a nonstick, ovenproof frying pan, add the spring onions and sweet potato slices and cook for 2 minutes.

Stir the coriander into the eggs, season well with pepper and pour into the pan. Arrange the goats' cheese slices on top and cook for a further 3–4 minutes until almost set.

Put the pan under a preheated medium-high grill and cook for 2–3 minutes until the top of the frittata is golden and bubbling. Serve with a crisp green salad.

COOK'S NOTES Sweet potato and goats' cheese are a wonderful combination; they work particularly well together in this quick and easy lunch or dinner recipe.

Preparation time:
10 minutes

Cooking time:
20 minutes

Serves: **2**

Oven temperature:
200°C (400°F) Gas Mark 6

1 teaspoon olive oil
3 baby leeks, thinly sliced
100 g (3½ oz) can green lentils, drained and rinsed
25 g (1 oz) feta cheese, crumbled
1 egg
6 tablespoons milk, plus extra for brushing
6 sheets of filo pastry, each 15 cm (6 inches) square, defrosted if frozen
salad, to serve

Heat the oil in a nonstick frying pan, add the leeks and cook for 3–4 minutes until softened. Stir in the lentils and half the feta.

Whisk the remaining feta, egg and milk in a bowl.

Brush the filo pastry squares with a little milk and use them to line 2 x 10 cm (4 inch) fluted flan tins. Divide the leek mixture between the tins and pour over the egg mixture.

Transfer the tins to a baking sheet and bake in a preheated oven, 200°C (400°F), Gas Mark 6, for 15 minutes or until the filling is set. Serve hot with salad.

Preparation time:
15 minutes

Cooking time:
10–12 minutes

Serves: **4**

Oven temperature:
200°C (400°F) Gas Mark 6

4 sheets of filo pastry, each 25 cm (10 inches) square, defrosted if frozen
1 tablespoon olive oil, plus extra for oiling
20 cherry tomatoes, halved
200 g (7 oz) goats' cheese, cut into 1 cm (½ inch) cubes
20 g (¾ oz) pine nuts
2 teaspoons chopped thyme leaves
salt and pepper
green salad, to serve

Lightly oil 4 x 10 cm (4 inch) individual tartlet tins. Brush a sheet of filo pastry with a little of the oil. Cut in half, then across into 4 equal-sized squares and use these to line one of the tins. Repeat with the remaining pastry. Brush any remaining oil over the pastry cases.

Put 5 tomato halves in the base of each tart. Top with the cheese, then add the remaining tomato halves and pine nuts. Sprinkle with the thyme leaves and season well with salt and pepper.

Bake the tarts in a preheated oven, 200°C (400°F), Gas Mark 6, for 10–12 minutes or until crisp and golden. Serve hot with a green salad.

COOK'S NOTES This would make a lovely dinner party dish for vegetarian guests. Filo pastry is light and delicate but very versatile and can used for any number of sweet and savoury recipes.

COOK'S NOTES You can prepare the tarts in advance and then just cook them when you're ready to serve. Try dry roasting the pine nuts for a minute before adding them to the tarts – this will give a rich, smoky flavour.

135 Wild mushroom filo baskets

Preparation time:
15 minutes

Cooking time:
15 minutes

Serves: **2**

Oven temperature:
180°C (350°F) Gas Mark 4

4 tablespoons avocado oil
1 red onion, chopped
375 g (12 oz) oyster mushrooms, stalks
  finely chopped and tops trimmed
50 g (2 oz) pine nuts
2 garlic cloves, chopped
25 ml (1 fl oz) brandy or whisky
50 ml (2 fl oz) vegetable stock
1 tablespoon soy sauce
4 sheets of filo pastry, each 30 cm
  (12 inches) square, defrosted if frozen
125 ml (4 fl oz) soya cream
1 tablespoon sweet chilli sauce, plus
  extra for drizzling
1 tablespoon maple syrup (optional)

TO SERVE
steamed mangetout
boiled brown basmati rice

Heat 2 tablespoons of oil in a saucepan, add the onion, mushrooms, pine nuts and garlic and cook until golden brown. Stir in the brandy or whisky, stock and soy sauce. Remove from the heat and set aside.

Lay a filo pastry sheet on a work surface and brush lightly with a little of the remaining oil. Put a second sheet on top and brush lightly with oil. Cut the double thickness in half and put one half in a diamond shape over the other half, to make a star shape with 8 points. Drape the prepared pastry over a small baking potato wrapped in foil. Brush the pastry lightly with oil and put on a baking sheet. Repeat with the remaining pastry sheets until you have 4 filo baskets. Bake in a preheated oven, 180°C (350°F), Gas Mark 4, for 10 minutes.

Stir 75 ml (3 fl oz) of the soya cream into the mushroom mixture, followed by the chilli sauce and maple syrup, if using. Return to a simmer. Lift the baskets from their supports, then fill with the mushroom mixture. Add drizzles of the remaining soya cream and chilli sauce to each basket. Serve with steamed mangetout and brown basmati rice.

136 Cherry tomato tarts with pesto

Preparation time:
10 minutes

Cooking time:
20 minutes

Serves: **4**

Oven temperature:
220°C (425°F) Gas Mark 7

2 tablespoons olive oil, plus extra for
  oiling
1 onion, finely chopped
375 g (12 oz) cherry tomatoes
2 garlic cloves, crushed
3 tablespoons sun-dried tomato paste
325 g (11 oz) ready-made puff pastry,
  defrosted if frozen
plain flour, for dusting
beaten egg, to glaze
150 g (5 oz) crème fraîche
2 tablespoons pesto
salt and pepper
basil leaves, to garnish

Heat the oil in a frying pan, add the onion and cook for 3 minutes. Halve about 150 g (5 oz) of the tomatoes. Remove the pan from the heat, add the garlic and sun-dried tomato paste, then stir in all the tomatoes.

Roll out the pastry on a lightly floured surface and cut out 4 rounds, each 12 cm (5 inch) across, using a plain cutter or small bowl. Transfer to an oiled baking sheet. Use a sharp knife to make a shallow mark about 1 cm (½ inch) from the edge of each round to form a rim. Brush the rims with beaten egg.

Pile the tomato mixture in the centres of the pastry cases within the rims. Bake in a preheated oven, 220°C (425°F), Gas Mark 7, for 15 minutes or until risen and golden.

Meanwhile, lightly mix the crème fraîche, pesto and salt and pepper to taste in a bowl so that the crème fraîche is streaked with the pesto. Transfer the cooked tarts to serving plates and spoon over the pesto sauce. Garnish with basil leaves and serve.

137 Devilled tofu and mushrooms

Preparation time:	½ teaspoon cornflour
10 minutes	juice of 1 large orange
	2 tablespoons mango chutney
Cooking time:	2 tablespoons Worcestershire sauce
12 minutes	1 tablespoon wholegrain mustard
	125 g (4 oz) firm tofu
Serves: 2	40 g (1½ oz) butter
	375 g (12 oz) large flat mushrooms
	2 chunky slices of wholegrain bread, toasted
	salt
	chopped parsley, to serve

Blend the cornflour with a little of the orange juice in a small bowl until smooth. Add the chutney, chopping up any large pieces, together with the Worcestershire sauce, mustard and the remaining orange juice.

Pat the tofu dry with kitchen paper and cut it into 1 cm (½ inch) dice. Melt the butter in a frying pan, add the tofu and cook for 3–5 minutes until golden all over. Remove the tofu with a slotted spoon. Add the mushrooms to the pan and cook for 5 minutes.

Return the tofu to the pan with the orange juice mixture and cook gently, stirring, for 2 minutes until the sauce is slightly thickened and bubbling. Season to taste with salt and pepper and spoon over the hot toast. Garnish with chopped parsley to serve.

138 Gingered tofu and mango salad

Preparation time:	125 g (4 oz) firm tofu
15 minutes, plus	25 g (1 oz) fresh root ginger, peeled and grated
marinating	2 tablespoons light soy sauce
Cooking time:	1 garlic clove, crushed
about 5 minutes	1 tablespoon seasoned rice vinegar
	2 tablespoons groundnut or soya oil
Serves: 2	1 bunch of spring onions, diagonally sliced into 1.5 cm (¾ inch) lengths
	40 g (1½ oz) cashew nuts
	1 small mango, halved, stoned and sliced
	½ small iceberg lettuce, shredded
	2 tablespoons water

Pat the tofu dry with kitchen paper and cut into 1 cm (½ inch) cubes. Mix together the ginger, soy sauce, garlic and vinegar in a small bowl. Add the tofu and toss the ingredients together. Cover and leave to marinate for 10 minutes.

Lift the tofu from the marinade with a fork, drain and reserve the marinade. Heat the oil in a frying pan, add the tofu and cook for 3–5 minutes or until golden all over. Remove with a slotted spoon and keep warm. Add the spring onions and cashew nuts to the pan and cook quickly for 30 seconds. Add the mango slices and cook for 30 seconds until heated through.

Pile the shredded lettuce on to serving plates and scatter the tofu and mango mixture over the top. Heat the reserved marinade in the pan with the measured water, pour over the salad and serve immediately.

COOK'S NOTES Use a really chunky, grainy bread for the toast so that it absorbs all the sweet and spicy devilled sauce.

139 Sizzling tofu with sesame greens

140 Marinated tofu with pak choi

Preparation time:
5 minutes, plus soaking

Cooking time:
10 minutes

Serves: **4**

250 g (8 oz) firm tofu, chilled
4 teaspoons sesame oil
3 tablespoons soy sauce
3 tablespoons sesame seeds
4 teaspoons sunflower oil
3.5 cm (1½ inch) piece of fresh root
ginger, peeled and finely chopped
2 garlic cloves, finely chopped
2 shallots, halved and thinly sliced
2 x 250 g (8 oz) packs of exotic baby
leaves and sprouts, including peanut
sprouts, pak choi, Swiss chard and
asparagus tips
1 tablespoon rice vinegar

Cut the tofu into 8 slices and arrange in a single layer in a shallow dish. Make diagonal cuts all over the tofu and sprinkle with half the sesame oil and half the soy sauce. Cover and leave to soak for 15 minutes, then drain, reserving the marinade.

Heat a wok or large, nonstick frying pan until hot, add the sesame seeds and cook, stirring, for 2–3 minutes until lightly browned. Remove from the heat, pour the reserved marinade over the top and quickly cover. When the seeds have stopped popping, stir and tip the seeds into a dish.

Wash and dry the pan, then add the sunflower oil and the remaining sesame oil and heat. Add the ginger, garlic and shallots and stir-fry for 2 minutes. Add the baby leaves and sprouts and stir-fry for 2–3 minutes until just wilted. Stir in the vinegar and remaining soy sauce.

Meanwhile, cook the tofu under a preheated high grill, turning once, for 4–5 minutes or until browned.

Spoon the leaf and sprout mixture on to plates and top with the grilled tofu and toasted sesame seeds and serve.

Preparation time:
10 minutes, plus marinating

Cooking time:
about 7 minutes

Serves: **1**

125 g (4 oz) firm tofu, cubed
1 garlic clove, crushed
1 teaspoon sesame oil
1 tablespoon soy sauce
1 red chilli, sliced
1 tablespoon chopped fresh coriander
2 pak choi, quartered lengthways
3 spring onions, sliced
boiled noodles, to serve

Put the tofu in a non-reactive bowl with the garlic, half the oil, the soy sauce, chilli and coriander. Toss thoroughly, then cover and leave to marinate for 10 minutes.

Heat the remaining oil in a nonstick frying pan. Lift the tofu from the marinade with a fork, drain and reserve the marinade. Add the tofu to the pan and stir-fry for 2 minutes. Add the pak choi and stir-fry for 3–4 minutes until tender. Add the reserved marinade and heat through. Serve immediately with noodles.

COOK'S NOTES Tofu is made from soya, which has many health benefits and so is a good choice for vegetarians. Although it has a rather bland flavour, tofu is delicious when marinated and cooked in a stir-fry.

141 Baked polenta with fontina

Preparation time:
10 minutes

Cooking time:
20 minutes

Serves: **4**

Oven temperature:
200°C (400°F) Gas Mark 6

150 g (5 oz) quick-cooking polenta
600 ml (1 pint) simmering water
125 g (4 oz) butter, plus extra for greasing
handful of marjoram, chopped
200 g (7 oz) fontina cheese, grated
salt and pepper

SAUCE
3 tablespoons olive oil
2 garlic cloves, crushed
1 onion, chopped
400 g (13 oz) can chopped tomatoes
1 thyme sprig
1 teaspoon white wine vinegar
1 teaspoon sugar

To make the sauce, heat the oil in a saucepan, add the garlic and onion and cook for 3 minutes. Add the tomatoes, thyme, vinegar, sugar and salt and pepper to taste and simmer for 10 minutes until reduced.

Meanwhile, pour the polenta into the saucepan of simmering measured water and beat well with a wooden spoon until thick and smooth. Reduce the heat and cook, stirring constantly, for 6–8 minutes, or according to the packet instructions.

Remove from the heat and stir in the butter, marjoram and salt and pepper to taste. Transfer the polenta to a chopping board, roll out to 1.5 cm (¾ inch) thick and leave for 5 minutes until set. Alternatively, shape into a loaf shape and cut into 1.5 cm (¾ inch) thick slices.

Butter a shallow ovenproof dish, cut the polenta into squares and line the bottom of the dish with half the squares. Sprinkle over half the fontina. Spoon over half the sauce and top with the remaining polenta. Add the remaining sauce and the remaining fontina and bake in a preheated oven, 200°C (400°F), Gas Mark 6, for 10 minutes until the cheese is golden and the sauce is bubbling.

142 Aubergine and mozzarella stacks

Preparation time:
10 minutes

Cooking time:
15 minutes

Serves: **4**

Oven temperature:
190°C (375°F) Gas Mark 5

1 aubergine, cut into 8 slices
4 beef tomatoes, skinned and cut into 8 slices
250 g (8 oz) packet of buffalo mozzarella, drained and cut into 8 slices
2 tablespoons olive oil, plus extra for oiling
salt and pepper
mint sprigs, to garnish
pesto, to serve

Heat a ridged griddle pan until smoking. Add the aubergine slices in a single layer and cook for 2–3 minutes until the undersides are browned. Turn them over and brown on the other side. Alternatively, cook under a preheated high grill.

Put 4 of the aubergine slices on a lightly oiled baking sheet. Put a tomato slice and a mozzarella slice on each one, then make a second layer of aubergine, tomato and mozzarella, sprinkling each layer with salt and pepper to taste as you go. Skewer with a cocktail stick through the centre to hold the stacks together.

Bake the stacks in a preheated oven, 190°C (375°F), Gas Mark 5, for 10 minutes.

Transfer the stacks to individual serving plates and carefully remove the cocktail sticks. Drizzle with the oil and top with a spoonful of pesto. Serve warm or at room temperature, garnished with mint sprigs.

143 Gnocchi with spinach and cheese

144 Macaroni cheese

Preparation time:	500 g (1 lb) ready-made gnocchi
10 minutes	250 g (8 oz) frozen leaf spinach, defrosted
	250 g (8 oz) mascarpone cheese
Cooking time:	50 g (2 oz) dolcelatte cheese
about 10 minutes	pinch of freshly grated nutmeg
	2 tablespoons freshly grated Parmesan
Serves: 4	cheese
	salt and pepper

Bring a large saucepan of lightly salted water to the boil. Add the gnocchi, return to the boil and cook for 3–4 minutes, or according to the packet instructions. Drain well and return to the pan.

Meanwhile, drain the spinach, using your hands to squeeze out all the excess water, and roughly chop. Stir into the cooked gnocchi with the mascarpone, dolcelatte and nutmeg. Stir gently until creamy and season to taste with salt and pepper.

Spoon the spinach mixture into a shallow, heatproof dish, sprinkle over the Parmesan and cook under a preheated high grill for 5–6 minutes until bubbling and golden.

Preparation time:	250 g (8 oz) dried macaroni
10 minutes	2 tablespoons extra virgin olive oil
	1 onion, finely chopped
Cooking time:	2 garlic cloves, crushed
20 minutes	2 teaspoons chopped rosemary
	125 g (4 oz) vegetarian bacon, diced
Serves: 4	(optional)
	200 ml (7 fl oz) single cream
Oven temperature:	200 ml (7 fl oz) milk
230°C (450°F) Gas Mark 8	200 g (7 oz) Cheddar cheese, grated
	salt and pepper
	green salad, to serve (optional)

Bring a large saucepan of lightly salted water to the boil. Add the pasta, return to the boil and cook for 10 minutes, or according to the packet instructions, until tender but still firm to the bite. Drain well.

Meanwhile, heat the oil in a large saucepan, add the onion, garlic, rosemary and bacon, if using, and cook for 5 minutes. Add the cream and milk and bring to boiling point. Remove the pan from the heat and stir in two-thirds of the cheese. Season to taste with salt and pepper.

Stir in the cooked macaroni and divide it among 4 small ovenproof dishes. Scatter over the remaining cheese and bake in a preheated oven, 230°C (450°F), Gas Mark 8, for 10 minutes or until bubbling and golden. Leave to cool slightly then serve with a crisp green salad, if you like.

COOK'S NOTES Ready-made gnocchi make a great, ultra-quick alternative to pasta. For a special occasion, divide the little potato dumplings and the spinach and cheese sauce among individual gratin dishes and grill for 3–4 minutes until golden and bubbling.

COOK'S NOTES This hearty dish includes vegetarian bacon, which is widely available in health food shops and larger supermarkets. It makes a good substitute for the real thing, but for vegetarians who prefer not to eat meat substitutes, the bacon can be omitted.

145 Polenta chips with saffron mushrooms

Preparation time:
10 minutes, plus infusing

Cooking time:
20 minutes

Serves: **4**

1 teaspoon saffron threads
1 tablespoon boiling water
500 g (1 lb) ready-cooked polenta
1 tablespoon plain flour
2 teaspoons chilli powder
vegetable oil, for shallow-frying
25 g (1 oz) butter
1 onion, chopped
2 garlic cloves, crushed
400 g (13 oz) mixed wild and cultivated
  mushrooms, halved if large
250 g (8 oz) mascarpone cheese
2 tablespoons chopped tarragon
finely grated rind and juice of ½ lemon
salt and pepper

Put the saffron threads in a small bowl with the measured water and leave to infuse until required.

Cut the polenta into 1 cm (½ inch) slices, then cut the slices into 1 cm (½ inch) chips. Mix the flour, chilli powder and salt and pepper to taste in a bowl and use to coat the polenta.

Heat 1 cm (½ inch) oil in a frying pan, add the polenta chips, half at a time, and fry for 10 minutes or until golden. Remove with a slotted spoon and drain on kitchen paper. Keep the polenta chips warm in a low oven while you cook the remainder.

Meanwhile, heat the butter in a separate frying pan, add the onion and garlic and cook for 5 minutes. Stir in the mushrooms and cook for 2 minutes. Add the mascarpone, tarragon, lemon rind and juice and the saffron and its soaking liquid and season to taste with salt and pepper. Stir until the mascarpone has melted. Serve with the polenta chips.

COOK'S NOTES Cooked polenta comes in rectangular blocks that can be sliced and then grilled, fried or baked. It is made from cornmeal and is used extensively in Italian cuisine.

146 Rice noodle and vegetable stir-fry

Preparation:
10 minutes

Cooking time:
10 minutes

Serves: **2**

50 g (2 oz) dried rice noodles
1 dessertspoon coconut oil
1 red onion, sliced
250 g (8 oz) rehydrated soya chunks or
  tofu
2 tablespoons soy sauce
1 teaspoon finely chopped fresh root
  ginger
1 garlic clove, finely chopped
125 g (4 oz) cabbage, finely sliced
125 g (4 oz) bean sprouts
8 lychees, peeled, stoned and quartered
1 dessertspoon blackstrap molasses

TO SERVE
nori flakes
sesame seeds
lime wedges (optional)

Soak the noodles in a saucepan of lightly salted boiling water for 4 minutes, then rinse under cold running water and drain.

Heat a wok or large frying pan until smoking, add the oil and then the onion and soya or tofu and stir-fry until golden all over. Pour in the soy sauce and stir to coat the mixture.

Reduce the heat, add all the remaining ingredients, including the noodles, and toss thoroughly until all the ingredients are well combined and heated through.

Transfer the stir-fry to warmed serving bowls, sprinkle with the nori flakes and sesame seeds and serve with lime wedges, if you like.

147 Thai vegetable curry

148 Rice pancakes with ginger sauce

Preparation time:
10 minutes

Cooking time:
15 minutes

Serves: **1**

1 teaspoon groundnut or vegetable oil
1 small onion, sliced
1 small green pepper, cored, deseeded and chopped
1 small red pepper, cored, deseeded and chopped
3 baby aubergines, halved, or 125 g (4 oz) large aubergine, chopped
3 baby courgettes, halved lengthways, or 1 medium courgette, chopped
75 g (3 oz) shiitake mushrooms
1 teaspoon green Thai curry paste
150 ml (¼ pint) coconut milk
100 ml (3½ fl oz) vegetable stock
1 tablespoon chopped fresh coriander
boiled rice, to serve

Heat the oil in a nonstick frying pan, add the onion, peppers, aubergines, courgettes and mushrooms and cook for 5–6 minutes until all the vegetables are beginning to soften.

Stir in the curry paste and cook, stirring, for 1 minute. Pour in the coconut milk and stock and bring to the boil. Reduce the heat and simmer for 5 minutes. Stir through the coriander and serve immediately with rice.

COOK'S NOTES Thai curries generally take less time to prepare and cook than Indian ones do, so this recipe is a great choice for a quick meal. It's packed full of fresh vegetables so it's good for you, too.

Preparation time:
15 minutes, plus softening

Cooking time:
5 minutes

Serves: **4**

SAUCE
1 garlic clove, roughly chopped
5 cm (2 inch) piece of fresh root ginger, peeled and roughly chopped
3 tablespoons light muscovado sugar
4 teaspoons soy sauce
5 teaspoons wine or rice vinegar
2 tablespoons tomato purée
2 tablespoons sesame seeds, plus extra to garnish

PANCAKES
8 rice pancakes
2 carrots, finely shredded
100 g (3½ oz) bean sprouts or mixed sprouting beans
small handful of mint, roughly chopped
1 celery stick, thinly sliced
4 spring onions, thinly sliced diagonally
1 tablespoon soy sauce

Put all the sauce ingredients, except the sesame seeds, in a blender or food processor and blend to a thin paste. Alternatively, crush the garlic, grate the ginger and whisk with the remaining ingredients. Stir in the sesame seeds and transfer to a serving bowl.

Soften the rice pancakes according to the packet instructions. Meanwhile, mix together the carrots, bean sprouts or sprouting beans, mint, celery, spring onions and soy sauce in a large bowl.

Divide the mixture evenly among the pancakes, spooning some into the centre of each. Fold in the bottom edge of each pancake to the centre, then roll it up from one side to the other to form a pocket.

Steam the pancakes in a vegetable or bamboo steamer for 5 minutes until heated through or put them on a wire rack set over a roasting tin of boiling water and cover with foil. Serve with the sauce, garnished with sesame seeds.

Preparation time:
10 minutes

Cooking time:
10 minutes

Serves: **4**

175 g (6 oz) green beans, trimmed and halved
2 tablespoons vegetable oil
1 onion, finely chopped
2 garlic cloves, crushed
400 g (13 oz) can plum tomatoes
2 tablespoons tomato purée
1 teaspoon dried mixed herbs
¼–½ teaspoon sugar
400 g (13 oz) can cannellini beans, drained and rinsed
2 tablespoons chopped basil, plus extra to garnish
salt and pepper

Blanch the green beans in a saucepan of lightly salted boiling water for 2 minutes. Drain, rinse immediately under cold running water and drain again.

Heat the oil in a saucepan, add the onion and garlic and cook for 2–3 minutes. Add the tomatoes and break them up with a wooden spoon. Add the tomato purée, herbs, sugar and salt and pepper to taste. Bring to the boil, stirring constantly.

Add the green and cannellini beans to the pan and toss until they are heated through and coated in the sauce. Remove the pan from the heat and stir in the basil. Taste and adjust the seasoning, if necessary. Serve immediately, garnished with basil.

Preparation time:
8 minutes

Cooking time:
22 minutes

Serves: **4**

3 tablespoons groundnut or vegetable oil
2 onions, chopped
2 small carrots, thinly sliced
3 garlic cloves, crushed
1 red pepper, cored, deseeded and chopped
2 bay leaves
1 tablespoon paprika
3 tablespoons tomato purée
400 ml (14 fl oz) can coconut milk
200 g (7 oz) can chopped tomatoes
150 ml (¼ pint) vegetable stock
400 g (13 oz) can red kidney beans, drained and rinsed
100 g (3½ oz) unsalted raw cashew nuts, toasted
small handful of fresh coriander, roughly chopped
salt and pepper
boiled rice, to serve

Heat the oil in a large saucepan, add the onions and carrots and cook for 3 minutes. Add the garlic, red pepper and bay leaves and cook for 5 minutes until the vegetables are soft and well browned.

Stir in the paprika, tomato purée, coconut milk, tomatoes, stock and beans and bring to the boil. Reduce the heat and simmer for 12 minutes until the vegetables are tender.

Stir in the cashew nuts and coriander, season to taste with salt and pepper and heat through for 2 minutes. Serve with rice.

COOK'S NOTES Ring the changes with the ingredients if you like, using different kinds of canned beans or substituting another fresh vegetable, such as mangetout or baby corn cobs, for the green beans.

151 Baby squash with red bean sauce

152 Wild rice with feta and orange

Preparation time:
10 minutes

Cooking time:
about 20 minutes

Serves: **4**

600 ml (1 pint) vegetable stock
1 kg (2 lb) mixed baby squash, such as gem, butternut or acorn
125 g (4 oz) baby spinach leaves

SAUCE
4 tablespoons olive oil
4 garlic cloves, thinly sliced
1 red pepper, cored, deseeded and finely chopped
2 tomatoes, chopped
400 g (13 oz) can red kidney beans, drained and rinsed
1–2 tablespoons hot chilli sauce, to taste
small handful of fresh coriander, chopped
salt

TO SERVE
steamed white rice
soured cream (optional)

Pour the stock into a saucepan and bring to the boil. Meanwhile, quarter and deseed the squash. Add to the stock, then reduce the heat, cover and simmer for 15 minutes or until the squash is just tender.

To make the sauce, heat the oil in a frying pan, add the garlic and red pepper and cook for 5 minutes. Add the tomatoes, beans, chilli sauce and a little salt and simmer for 5 minutes until pulpy.

Drain the squash from the stock, reserving the stock, and return it to the pan. Scatter over the spinach leaves, cover and cook for 1 minute or until the spinach has wilted.

Pile the vegetables on to steamed rice on serving plates. Stir 8 tablespoons of the reserved stock into the sauce with the coriander. Spoon over the vegetables and serve with soured cream, if you like.

Preparation time:
15 minutes

Cooking time:
No cooking

Serves: **1**

150 g (5 oz) cold cooked mixed long-grain and wild rice
25 g (1 oz) feta cheese, crumbled
2 tomatoes, chopped
15 g (½ oz) toasted mixed seeds, such as pumpkin, sesame and sunflower
2 oranges

Put the rice, feta, tomatoes and seeds into a bowl and toss together.

Squeeze the juice from 1 orange into the bowl. Working over the bowl to catch the juice, remove the peel and pith from the remaining orange, then cut between the membranes to remove the segments.

Add the orange segments to the bowl and toss well to mix. Serve immediately.

COOK'S NOTES Wild rice isn't actually rice at all: it's the grain of a grass grown in lakes and marshes. It has a lovely nutty flavour and works well when mixed with regular rice.

6 Fish and Shellfish

153 Mullet with orange and olive salad

154 Spiced swordfish with fennel salad

Preparation time:
15 minutes, plus soaking

Cooking time:
5 minutes

Serves: **4**

3 large oranges
50 g (2 oz) raisins
¼ teaspoon ground cinnamon
5 tablespoons extra virgin olive oil, plus extra to serve (optional)
large handful of flat leaf parsley
100 g (3½ oz) green olives
4 red mullet fillets, about 150 g (5 oz) each
salt and pepper

Squeeze the juice from 1 orange into a bowl and add the raisins, cinnamon and 4 tablespoons of the oil. Leave to soak for 10 minutes.

Remove the peel and pith from the remaining oranges, then cut between the membranes to remove the segments, cutting them in half if large. Put the segments in a large bowl. Pick the leaves from the parsley and add to the orange segments with the olives. Season to taste with salt and pepper.

Brush the mullet fillets with the remaining oil and season to taste with salt and pepper on both sides. Heat a heavy-based frying pan until hot, add the fillets, skin-side down, and cook for 2 minutes. Turn them over and cook for a further 2 minutes. Transfer the mullet to serving plates and leave to rest briefly.

Add the orange juice mixture to the orange and olive salad, toss well and serve with the mullet. Drizzle with a little extra oil, if you like.

Preparation time:
10 minutes

Cooking time:
5 minutes

Serves: **4**

2 teaspoons crushed coriander seeds
4 swordfish steaks, about 200 g (7 oz) each
4–6 tablespoons extra virgin olive oil
1 large fennel bulb, trimmed
1 garlic clove, thinly sliced
2 tablespoons baby capers in salt, rinsed
handful of mint leaves
1–2 tablespoons lemon juice
salt and pepper
rocket leaves, to serve

Mix the crushed coriander seeds with some salt and pepper. Brush the swordfish fillets with a little of the oil and rub over the spice mix.

Remove the tough outer layer of fennel and discard. Cut the bulb in half lengthways and then crossways into wafer-thin slices. Put it in a bowl with the garlic, capers, mint leaves, the remaining oil and lemon juice. Season to taste with salt and pepper.

Heat a ridged griddle pan until smoking. Add the swordfish and cook for 1½ minutes on each side. Remove from the pan, wrap loosely in foil and leave to rest for 5 minutes.

Serve the swordfish and any juices from the pan with the fennel salad and rocket leaves.

COOK'S NOTES This pretty, refreshing dish is perfect for laid-back summertime entertaining. When cooking small fish fillets, always fry them skin side down first to prevent the fish from curling up in the pan. You could also use other fish fillets such as bream or trout.

COOK'S NOTES Swordfish is a wonderfully meaty fish, which requires only a short cooking time; if you overcook this type of fish, it can become dry and tough. It's also a good idea to let your fish rest, like meat, before eating to maximize its moistness and tenderness.

155 Grilled snapper with salmoriglio

156 Lemon sole with caper sauce

Preparation time:
10 minutes

Cooking time:
10–15 minutes

Serves: **4**

4 red snapper, about 375 g (12 oz) each, scaled and gutted, heads and tails removed
150 ml (¼ pint) extra virgin olive oil
4 tablespoons lemon juice
2 garlic cloves, crushed
2 tablespoons chopped parsley
1 teaspoon dried oregano
salt and pepper

TO SERVE
tomato, red onion, olive and basil salad
crusty bread

Preparation time:
10 minutes

Cooking time:
10 minutes

Serves: **2**

2 lemon sole, about 300 g (10 oz) each, skinned
extra virgin olive oil spray
65 g (2½ oz) butter
4 tablespoons baby capers, drained and rinsed
1 tablespoon chopped parsley
1 tablespoon chopped chives
2 tablespoons lemon juice
salt and pepper
steamed carrot and courgette batons, to serve

Using a sharp knife, make 4 slashes in each side of each fish. Season to taste with salt and pepper and brush all over with a little of the oil.

Heat a ridged griddle pan until hot. Add the fish and cook for 5–7 minutes on each side until cooked through. Alternatively, cook under a preheated high grill.

Meanwhile, whisk together the remaining oil, the lemon juice, garlic and herbs in a bowl and season to taste with salt and pepper. Transfer the cooked fish to a large warmed platter and spoon over the dressing. Cover loosely with foil and leave to rest for 5 minutes.

Serve with a tomato, red onion, olive and basil salad and crusty bread.

Spray the lemon sole with oil and season well with salt and pepper on both sides. Put them in a foil-lined grill pan and cook under a preheated high grill for 3 minutes on each side. Transfer to warmed serving plates, cover with foil and leave to rest for 5 minutes.

Meanwhile, heat the butter in a saucepan, add the capers and cook gently, stirring, for 1 minute. Stir in the herbs, lemon juice and pepper to taste, then remove from the heat.

Pour the sauce over the sole and serve immediately with steamed carrot and courgette batons.

COOK'S NOTES In spite of its simplicity, this dish of red snapper, served with the classic Italian garlic and lemon sauce, salmoriglio, is sure to impress your dinner party guests. Serve with plenty of crusty bread for mopping up the delicious juices.

157 Salmon trout and shiitake parcels

Preparation time: **10 minutes**	**4 salmon trout or salmon fillets, about 150 g (5 oz) each** **100 g (3½ oz) shiitake mushrooms** **8 spring onions, sliced**
Cooking time: **6–7 minutes**	**75 g (3 oz) butter, cut into 4 cubes** **4 tablespoons sake or dry sherry** **4 tablespoons light soy sauce** **steamed vegetables, to serve**
Serves: **4**	
Oven temperature: **180°C (350°F) Gas Mark 4**	

Cut 4 pieces of foil about 25 cm (10 inches) square. Put a salmon trout or salmon fillet in the centre of each. Divide the mushrooms and spring onions among the fillets and add a cube of butter to each.

Pull the edges of the foil squares up around the fish and drizzle over the sake or sherry. Bring the edges of each foil square up to meet and fold over tightly to seal the parcels.

Transfer the parcels to a baking sheet and bake in a preheated oven, 180°C (350°F), Gas Mark 4, for 6–7 minutes. Carefully open the parcels and drizzle in the soy sauce. Serve with steamed vegetables, such as pak choi, baby corn cobs, courgettes and carrots.

COOK'S NOTES You could use any fish you want for this recipe, but salmon trout goes particularly well with the flavours of sake and soy sauce and the texture of the mushrooms.

158 Swordfish with sage crumb

Preparation time: **10 minutes**	**5 tablespoons extra virgin olive oil, plus extra to serve** **2 garlic cloves, chopped** **2 tablespoons chopped sage**
Cooking time: **10 minutes**	**125 g (4 oz) fresh white breadcrumbs finely grated rind and juice of 1 lemon** **250 g (8 oz) fine green beans, trimmed**
Serves: **4**	**4 swordfish fillets, about 200 g (7 oz) each**

Heat 4 tablespoons of the oil in a frying pan, add the garlic, sage, breadcrumbs and lemon rind and cook for 5 minutes until crisp and golden. Drain thoroughly on kitchen paper.

Bring a saucepan of lightly salted water to the boil, add the beans and cook for 3 minutes until tender. Drain well, season to taste with salt and pepper and toss with a little of the lemon juice. Keep warm.

Meanwhile, brush the swordfish with the remaining oil and season to taste with salt and pepper. Heat a ridged griddle pan until smoking. Add the swordfish and cook for 1½ minutes on each side. Remove the fish from the pan, wrap loosely in foil and leave to rest for 5 minutes.

Transfer the swordfish to individual plates, drizzle with the remaining lemon juice and top with the breadcrumb mixture. Serve with the beans and drizzle with extra oil.

159 Maple and mustard glazed salmon

Preparation time:
5 minutes

Cooking time:
8–10 minutes

Serves: 4

2 tablespoons wholegrain mustard
1 tablespoon maple syrup
4 salmon fillets, skin on, about 125 g
**   (4 oz) each**
450 g (14½ oz) asparagus spears or
**   tender-stem broccoli, trimmed**
new potatoes, to serve

Mix the mustard with the maple syrup in a cup to make a glaze for the salmon.

Put the salmon fillets, skin side down, on a baking sheet or foil-lined grill rack and spread the glaze over the top. Place under a preheated medium grill and cook for 4–5 minutes on each side, depending on thickness, until just cooked through.

Meanwhile, steam the asparagus or broccoli until just tender. Transfer to 4 warmed plates, top with the salmon and serve with new potatoes.

160 Five-spice salmon with Asian greens

Preparation time:
10 minutes

Cooking time:
10 minutes

Serves: 4

2 teaspoons crushed black peppercorns
2 teaspoons Chinese five-spice powder
1 teaspoon salt
¼ teaspoon cayenne pepper
4 salmon fillets, about 200 g (7 oz) each,
**   skinned**
3 tablespoons sunflower oil
500 g (1 lb) choi sum or pak choi, sliced
3 garlic cloves, sliced
3 tablespoons rice wine or dry sherry
75 ml (3 fl oz) vegetable stock
2 tablespoons light soy sauce
1 teaspoon sesame oil
boiled rice, to serve

Mix together the crushed peppercorns, five-spice powder, salt and cayenne on a plate. Brush the salmon with a little of the sunflower oil and dust with the spice mixture.

Heat a griddle pan over a medium heat. Add the salmon and cook for 4 minutes. Turn it over and cook for a further 2–3 minutes until just cooked through. Transfer to a plate, cover loosely with foil and leave to rest for 5 minutes.

Meanwhile, heat the remaining sunflower oil in a wok or large frying pan, add the greens and stir-fry for 2 minutes. Add the garlic and stir-fry for a further 1 minute. Add the wine or sherry, stock, soy sauce and sesame oil and cook for a further 2 minutes until the greens are tender. Serve the salmon and greens with boiled rice.

COOK'S NOTES Fish is the perfect quick dish and it's a healthy option as well. This tasty salmon recipe is ready to serve in minutes, and the glaze will add a lovely colour and flavour to the fish.

161 Pan-fried halibut with papaya

162 Halibut parcels

161 Pan-fried halibut with papaya

Preparation time:
10 minutes

Cooking time:
about 15 minutes

Serves: **4**

2 teaspoons olive oil
3 garlic cloves, crushed
4 halibut steaks, about 625 g (1¼ lb)
in total
salt and pepper

SALSA
1 papaya, peeled, deseeded and cubed
½ red onion, finely chopped
15 g (½ oz) fresh coriander leaves, finely
chopped
¼–½ teaspoon chilli powder, to taste
1 red pepper, cored, deseeded and finely
chopped
juice of ½ lime

TO SERVE
watercress
lime wedges

Heat the oil in a large, nonstick frying pan, add the garlic and cook, stirring, for a few seconds. Add the halibut and cook for 10–12 minutes until just cooked, turning it halfway through cooking.

Meanwhile, to make the salsa, mix together all the ingredients in a bowl.

Serve the halibut on a bed of watercress, with the salsa and lime wedges on the side.

162 Halibut parcels

Preparation time:
15 minutes, plus infusing

Cooking time:
10 minutes

Serves: **4**

Oven temperature:
190°C (375°F) Gas Mark 5

4 tablespoons orange juice
pinch of saffron threads
4 halibut fillets, about 200 g (7 oz) each
2 tablespoons extra virgin olive oil
3 tomatoes, diced
2 garlic cloves, finely chopped
4 tablespoons dry sherry
4 basil sprigs
finely grated rind of ½ orange
salt and pepper
mashed potatoes, to serve

Put the orange juice and saffron threads in a bowl and leave to infuse until required.

Cut 4 large rectangles of foil and put a halibut fillet in the centre of each. Pull the edges of the foil up around the fish.

Divide the oil, tomatoes, garlic, sherry, basil, orange rind and saffron-infused orange juice among the fillets and season well with salt and pepper. Bring the edges of each foil rectangle up to meet and fold over tightly to seal the parcels.

Transfer the parcels to a baking sheet and bake in a preheated oven, 190°C (375°F), Gas Mark 5, for 10 minutes. Remove the parcels from the oven and leave to rest for 5 minutes. Carefully open the parcels and tip the contents on to warmed plates. Serve with mashed potatoes.

COOK'S NOTES This is an effortless way to cook fish, with the foil parcels trapping all the wonderful juices. Be careful when opening the parcels because the escaping steam will be hot.

163 Grilled sea bass with tomato sauce

Preparation time:
15 minutes

Cooking time:
about 15 minutes

Serves: **6**

1 tablespoon olive oil
1 onion, finely chopped
300 g (10 oz) cherry tomatoes, halved
2 large pinches of saffron threads
  (optional)
150 ml (¼ pint) dry white wine
125 ml (4 fl oz) fish stock
finely grated rind of 1 lemon
12 small sea bass fillets, about 100 g
  (3½ oz) each
1 teaspoon fennel seeds
salt and pepper
basil or oregano leaves, to garnish
  (optional)

Heat the oil in a frying pan, add the onion and cook for 5 minutes. Add the tomatoes, saffron, if using, wine and stock, then stir in the lemon rind and a little salt and pepper. Bring to the boil and cook for 2 minutes.

Pour the tomato mixture into the base of a foil-lined grill pan, add the lemon slices and set aside. Arrange the fish fillets, skin side up, on top. Spoon some of the tomato mixture over the skin, then sprinkle with salt and pepper to taste and the fennel seeds.

Cook the sea bass under a preheated high grill for 5–6 minutes until the skin is crisp and the fish flakes easily when pressed with a knife. Transfer the fillets to warmed serving plates and garnish with basil or oregano leaves, if you like, before serving.

164 Snapper with carrots and caraway

Preparation time:
10 minutes

Cooking time:
15 minutes

Serves: **4**

500 g (1 lb) carrots, sliced
2 teaspoons caraway seeds
4 red snapper fillets, about 175 g (6 oz)
  each
2 oranges
1 bunch of fresh coriander, roughly
  chopped, plus extra to garnish
4 tablespoons olive oil
salt and pepper

Heat a ridged griddle pan over a medium heat. Add the carrots and cook for 3 minutes on each side, adding the caraway seeds for the last 2 minutes of cooking. Transfer to a bowl and keep warm.

Add the snapper fillets to the pan and cook for 3 minutes on each side. Meanwhile, squeeze the juice from 1 of the oranges into a bowl. Cut the other orange into quarters. Add the orange quarters to the pan for the last 2 minutes of cooking and cook until charred.

Add the coriander to the carrots and mix well. Season to taste with salt and pepper and stir in the oil and orange juice. Serve the snapper with the carrots and griddled orange quarters, garnished with coriander.

COOK'S NOTES This dish is all cooked on a griddle pan, which is a really healthy way of cooking, as no fat is used and all the nutrients stay in the food. The orange juice adds a touch of sweetness.

165 Parmesan-crusted cod burger

Preparation time:
15 minutes

Cooking time:
10 minutes

Serves: **4**

1 egg
1 teaspoon English mustard powder
75 g (3 oz) fresh white breadcrumbs
2 tablespoons finely chopped basil
25 g (1 oz) Parmesan cheese, freshly grated
4 tablespoons plain flour
4 cod fillets, about 175 g (6 oz) each
2 tablespoons light olive oil
salt and pepper

TO SERVE
4 crusty poppy seed rolls
mixed salad leaves
1 beef tomato, sliced
4 tablespoons mayonnaise
lemon wedges

Beat the egg and mustard with a little salt and pepper in a bowl. Mix together the breadcrumbs, basil and Parmesan on a plate. Spread the flour out on a separate plate.

Coat the cod fillets in the flour. Dip them into the egg mixture, then press them into the breadcrumb mixture to coat evenly.

Heat the oil in a shallow saucepan, add the fish and cook for 4 minutes on each side until golden and cooked through. Meanwhile, halve the rolls horizontally and toast under a preheated grill.

Fill the toasted rolls with the salad leaves, tomato slices and crusted cod fillets. Serve with the lids on the side, accompanied by mayonnaise, lemon wedges and extra salad leaves.

COOK'S NOTES You can prepare these burgers in advance and keep them in the refrigerator until you're ready to cook. This makes them a great choice for kids when they come in from school.

166 Griddled salmon with a chilli crust

Preparation time:
10 minutes

Cooking time:
about 10 minutes

Serves: **4**

3 teaspoons crushed dried red chillies
3 tablespoons sesame seeds
1 large bunch of parsley, chopped
4 salmon fillets, about 150 g (5 oz) each, skinned
1 egg white, lightly beaten
salt and pepper

TO SERVE
2 limes, halved
boiled noodles (optional)

Heat a ridged griddle pan over a medium heat. Mix the crushed chillies, sesame seeds, parsley and salt and pepper to taste on a plate. Dip the salmon fillets into the egg white, then press them into the chilli mixture to coat evenly.

Add the salmon fillets to the pan and cook for 4 minutes on each side, turning them carefully with a spatula to keep the crust on the fish. Add the lime halves for the last 2 minutes of cooking and cook until charred.

Serve the salmon with the griddled lime halves, accompanied by noodles, if you like.

COOK'S NOTES This Asian-inspired recipe has a bit of a kick because of the dried chillies. If you are serving noodles with the salmon, drizzle over a little soy sauce for extra flavour.

Preparation time: **15 minutes**

Cooking time: **10 minutes**

Serves: **4**

4 monkfish fillets, about 150 g (5 oz) each
4 teaspoons black olive tapenade
8 basil leaves
**8 rashers of streaky bacon, stretched
   with the back of a knife**
125 ml (4 fl oz) balsamic vinegar
375 g (12 oz) green beans
125 g (4 oz) frozen peas
6 spring onions, finely sliced
125 g (4 oz) feta cheese, crumbled
2 tablespoons basil oil
salt

Lay the monkfish fillets on a chopping board and, using a sharp knife, make a deep incision about 5 cm (2 inches) long in the side of each fillet. Stuff each incision with 1 teaspoon tapenade and 2 basil leaves. Wrap 2 rashers of bacon around each fillet, sealing in the filling. Secure with a cocktail stick.

Heat a ridged griddle pan over a medium heat, add the monkfish fillets and cook for 4–5 minutes on each side or until cooked through. Remove from the pan and leave to rest for 1–2 minutes.

Meanwhile, pour the vinegar into a small saucepan. Bring it to the boil, then reduce the heat and simmer for 8–10 minutes until it is thick and glossy. Leave to cool slightly, but keep warm.

Bring a saucepan of salted water to the boil, add the beans and cook for 3 minutes. Add the peas and cook for a further minute. Drain, then toss the beans and peas with the spring onions, feta and basil oil.

Transfer the vegetable mixture to warmed serving plates. Top each pile with a monkfish fillet and serve immediately, drizzled with the warm balsamic dressing.

Preparation time: **15 minutes**

Cooking time: **5 minutes**

Serves: **2**

**10–12 prepared baby squid, about 375 g
   (12 oz) including tentacles**
4 limes, halved
mixed green leaf salad, to serve

DRESSING

2 red chillies, finely chopped
finely grated rind and juice of 2 limes
**2.5 cm (1 inch) piece of fresh root ginger,
   peeled and grated**
**100 g (3½ oz) dried, creamed or freshly
   grated coconut**
4 tablespoons groundnut oil
1–2 tablespoons chilli oil
1 tablespoon white wine vinegar

Cut down the side of each squid so that they can be laid flat. Using a sharp knife, score the inside flesh lightly in a crisscross pattern.

Mix all the dressing ingredients together in a bowl. Toss the squid in half the dressing until thoroughly coated.

Heat a ridged griddle pan until smoking, add the limes, cut side down, and cook for 2 minutes or until well charred. Remove from the pan and set aside.

Keeping the griddle pan very hot, add the squid and cook for 1 minute. Turn them over and cook for a further minute until charred. Transfer the squid to a chopping board and cut them into strips. Drizzle with the remaining dressing and serve immediately with the charred limes and a mixed green leaf salad.

COOK'S NOTES Be careful not to overcook the squid, because they will quickly go rubbery and taste unpleasant.

169 Grilled sardines with tomato salsa

170 Grilled haddock with lentils and spinach

Preparation time:
10 minutes

Cooking time:
3–4 minutes

Serves: **1**

2 fresh sardines, about 125 g (4 oz) in total, gutted
4 tablespoons lemon juice
1 tablespoon chopped parsley
salt and pepper
toasted ciabatta, to serve

TOMATO SALSA
8 cherry tomatoes, chopped
1 spring onion, sliced
1 tablespoon chopped basil
½ red pepper, cored, deseeded and chopped

Preparation time:
10 minutes

Cooking time:
about 15 minutes

Serves: **1**

1 teaspoon olive oil
½ onion, finely chopped
pinch of ground cumin
pinch of ground turmeric
pinch of dried red chilli flakes
125 g (4 oz) can lentils, drained and rinsed
75 g (3 oz) baby spinach leaves
2 tablespoons crème fraîche
1 skinless haddock fillet, about 125 g (4 oz)
lemon wedge, to garnish
grilled tomatoes, to serve

To make the tomato salsa, mix all the ingredients together in a bowl.

Put the sardines on a baking sheet and drizzle with the lemon juice. Season to taste with salt and pepper.

Cook the sardines under a preheated high grill, turning once, for 3–4 minutes until cooked through. Sprinkle with the chopped parsley and serve immediately with the tomato salsa and toasted ciabatta.

Heat half the oil in a nonstick frying pan, add the onion and cook for 3–4 minutes until softened. Add the cumin, turmeric and chilli flakes and cook, stirring, for 1 minute. Add the lentils, spinach and crème fraîche and cook gently for 3 minutes until the spinach has wilted.

Meanwhile, brush the haddock on each side with the remaining oil. Put the haddock on a nonstick baking sheet and cook under a preheated high grill for 2–3 minutes on each side until just cooked through.

Arrange the lentils and spinach mixture on a warmed serving plate and top with the haddock. Garnish with a lemon wedge and serve with grilled tomatoes.

COOK'S NOTES Sardines are an oily fish so they're packed full of beneficial omega-3 oils. The tomato salsa provides a crisp, light contrast to the fish and can also be used to accompany other dishes.

171 Baked trout parcel with tartare sauce

172 Griddled red snapper with steamed spinach

Preparation time:
10 minutes

Cooking time:
12–15 minutes

Serves: **1**

Oven temperature:
200°C (400°F) Gas Mark 6

**1 rainbow trout fillet, about 150 g (5 oz)
finely grated rind and juice of 1 lime
potatoes and green vegetables, to serve**

TARTARE SAUCE
**2 cocktail gherkins, finely chopped
1 teaspoon capers, roughly chopped
2 teaspoons crème fraîche
1 spring onion, sliced
1 tablespoon chopped parsley**

Cut a piece of foil about 25 cm (10 inches) square. Put the trout fillet in the centre and pull the edges of the foil up around the fish. Sprinkle with half the lime rind and juice. Bring the edges of the foil up to meet and fold over tightly to seal the parcel.

Transfer the parcel to a baking sheet and bake in a preheated oven, 200°C (400°F), Gas Mark 6, for 12–15 minutes.

Meanwhile, to make the tartare sauce, mix all the ingredients together in a small bowl and stir in the remaining lime rind and juice.

Carefully open the parcel and tip the contents on to a warmed plate. Serve the trout with the tartare sauce, accompanied by potatoes, green vegetables and carrots.

Preparation time:
5 minutes

Cooking time:
8 minutes

Serves: **4**

**4 red snapper fillets, about 175 g (6 oz)
each
250 g (8 oz) spinach
1 teaspoon pumpkin seeds
1 teaspoon sunflower seeds
2 teaspoons olive oil
1 bunch of spring onions, shredded, to
garnish**

Heat a griddle pan over a medium heat. Add the snapper fillets and cook for 4 minutes on each side.

Meanwhile, steam the spinach until just tender. Drain.

Mix the pumpkin seeds, sunflower seeds and oil with the spinach. Serve immediately with the snapper fillets, garnished with the shredded spring onions.

COOK'S NOTES This recipe would also work well on a barbecue as the foil keeps the fish intact and the steam helps to cook it. Make sure the fish is cooked through completely before serving.

173 Mackerel with lemon and olives

Preparation time:
15 minutes

Cooking time:
15 minutes

Serves: **4**

Oven temperature:
220°C (425°F) Gas Mark 7

**4 mackerel, about 300 g (10 oz) each,
    gutted and heads removed
1 small bunch of thyme, bruised
1 teaspoon cumin seeds, bruised
2 tablespoons extra virgin olive oil, plus
    extra for drizzling
1 lemon, sliced
2 bay leaves
125 g (4 oz) black olives
2 tablespoons lemon juice
salt and pepper
tomato, onion and basil salad, to serve**

Using a sharp knife, make 3 slashes in each side of each fish. Mix the thyme, cumin, oil and salt and pepper to taste in a bowl. Rub the mixture all over the fish, making sure that some of the flavourings are pressed into the cuts.

Arrange the mackerel in a roasting tin and scatter over the lemon slices, bay leaves and olives. Drizzle with the lemon juice and a little extra oil and season to taste with salt and pepper. Roast in a preheated oven, 220°C (425°F), Gas Mark 7, for 15 minutes until the fish are cooked through. Serve immediately with a tomato, onion and basil salad.

COOK'S NOTES Bruising the thyme and cumin seeds helps to release their flavour. The easiest way to do this is in a mortar with a pestle or on a chopping board with a rolling pin.

174 Roasted cod with prosciutto

Preparation time:
10 minutes

Cooking time:
15 minutes

Serves: **4**

Oven temperature:
220°C (425°) Gas Mark 7

**375 g (12 oz) cherry tomatoes, halved
50 g (2 oz) pitted black olives
2 tablespoons capers, drained and rinsed
finely grated rind and juice of 1 lemon
2 teaspoons chopped thyme
4 tablespoons extra virgin olive oil
4 cod fillets, about 175 g (6 oz) each
4 slices of prosciutto
salt and pepper
basil leaves, to garnish**

TO SERVE
**new potatoes
green salad**

Mix together the tomatoes, olives, capers, lemon rind, thyme and oil in a roasting tin and season to taste with salt and pepper. Arrange the cod fillets in the tin in a single layer, spooning some of the tomato mixture over the fish. Scatter the prosciutto over the top.

Roast in a preheated oven, 220°C (425°), Gas Mark 7, for 15 minutes. Remove from the oven and drizzle over the lemon juice. Cover loosely with foil and leave to rest for 5 minutes.

Serve the cod garnished with basil leaves and accompanied with new potatoes and a green salad.

COOK'S NOTES This attractive all-in-one dish is a great quick and easy solution to mid week entertaining.

175 Tuna and warm bean salad

176 Seared sesame tuna

Preparation time:
10 minutes

Cooking time:
10 minutes

Serves: **4**

4 tuna steaks, about 200 g (7 oz) each
100 ml (3½ fl oz) extra virgin olive oil,
  plus extra to serve
2 garlic cloves, crushed
2 teaspoons chopped rosemary leaves
pinch of dried red chilli flakes
2 x 400 g (13 oz) cans cannellini beans,
  drained and rinsed
4 plum tomatoes, deseeded and diced
½ red onion, finely chopped
1½ tablespoons red wine vinegar
2 tablespoons chopped parsley, plus
  extra leaves to garnish
salt and pepper

Preparation time:
10 minutes

Cooking time:
about 3 minutes

Serves: **4**

1 tablespoon black sesame seeds
1 tablespoon white sesame seeds
1 tuna steak, about 2.5 cm (1 inch) thick
  and 375 g (12 oz)
1 tablespoon sunflower oil
100 g (3½ oz) mixed herb or baby leaf
  salad
6 radishes, sliced
¼ cucumber, peeled and sliced

DRESSING
3 tablespoons light soy sauce
3 tablespoons mirin (Japanese rice wine)
1 tablespoon rice vinegar
½ teaspoon wasabi

Brush the tuna with a little of the oil and season to taste with salt and pepper. Heat 4 tablespoons of the remaining oil in a frying pan, add the garlic, rosemary and chilli flakes and cook for 1–2 minutes.

Add the beans, tomatoes and onion and season to taste with salt and pepper. Cook gently for 5 minutes until heated through. Remove the pan from the heat and stir in the remaining oil, the vinegar and chopped parsley.

Meanwhile, heat a heavy-based frying pan or ridged griddle pan until smoking. Add the tuna and cook for 45 seconds on each side until seared on the outside but still pink in the centre, or longer for a less-pink centre. Remove the tuna from the pan, wrap it loosely in foil and leave to rest for 5 minutes.

Spoon the bean mixture on to individual plates. Slice the tuna and arrange on top with any juices from the pan. Serve immediately, drizzled with a little extra oil.

Mix together all the dressing ingredients in a small bowl and set aside.

Mix the sesame seeds on a plate. Rub the tuna steak with the oil, then roll it in the sesame seeds to coat.

Heat a heavy-based frying pan or ridged griddle pan until smoking. Add the tuna and cook for 45 seconds on each side until seared on the outside but still pink in the centre, or longer for a less-pink centre. Remove the tuna from the pan, wrap it loosely in foil and leave to rest for 5 minutes, then slice it as thinly as you can.

Arrange the tuna on a serving platter, top with the herb or salad leaves, radishes and cucumber, then drizzle over the dressing.

COOK'S NOTES Tuna is best cooked so that the centre of the steak is still pink and juicy. You can cook it for a little longer if you prefer, but be careful not to overcook because it will become tough and dry.

177 Monkfish and prawn Thai curry

Preparation time:
15 minutes

Cooking time:
about 6 minutes

Serves: **4**

3 tablespoons green Thai curry paste
400 ml (14 fl oz) can coconut milk
1 lemon grass stalk, bruised (optional)
2 kaffir lime leaves, torn into pieces (optional)
1 tablespoon soft light brown sugar
1 teaspoon salt
300 g (10 oz) monkfish tail, cubed
75 g (3 oz) green beans, trimmed
12 raw tiger prawns, peeled and deveined
3 tablespoons Thai fish sauce
2 tablespoons lime juice
boiled rice, to serve

TO GARNISH
fresh coriander sprigs
sliced green chillies

Put the curry paste and coconut milk in a saucepan with the lemon grass and lime leaves, if using, sugar and salt. Bring to the boil and add the monkfish.

Reduce the heat and simmer gently for 2 minutes. Add the beans and cook for 2 minutes. Remove the pan from the heat and stir in the prawns, fish sauce and lime juice. The prawns will cook in the residual heat, but you will need to push them under the liquid.

Transfer the curry to a warmed serving dish and garnish with coriander sprigs and chilli slices. Serve with boiled rice.

COOK'S NOTES This recipe includes lemon grass and kaffir lime leaves for a real Thai flavour, but if you find a good-quality, authentic curry paste from Thailand, you can leave them out.

178 Mussel and lemon curry

Preparation time:
15 minutes

Cooking time:
15 minutes

Serves: **4**

1 kg (2 lb) live mussels, scrubbed and debearded
125 ml (4 fl oz) lager or beer
50 g (2 oz) unsalted butter
1 onion, chopped
1 garlic clove, crushed
2.5 cm (1 inch) piece of fresh root ginger, peeled and grated
1 tablespoon medium curry powder
150 ml (5 oz) single cream
2 tablespoons lemon juice
salt and pepper
chopped parsley, to garnish
crusty bread, to serve (optional)

Discard any mussels that are broken or do not close immediately when sharply tapped with a knife. Put them in a large saucepan with the beer, cover and cook, shaking the pan frequently, for 4 minutes until all the mussels have opened. Discard any that remain closed. Strain, reserving the cooking liquid. Keep the cooking liquid warm.

Meanwhile, melt the butter in a large saucepan, add the onion, garlic, ginger and curry powder and cook, stirring frequently, for 5 minutes. Strain in the reserved cooking liquid and bring to the boil. Boil until reduced by half. Whisk in the cream and lemon juice and simmer gently.

Stir in the mussels, warm through and season to taste with salt and pepper. Garnish the curry with chopped parsley and serve with crusty bread, if you like.

179 Prawn laksa

Preparation time: 15 minutes	**1 teaspoon olive oil**
	½ red pepper, cored, deseeded and sliced
	100 g (3½ oz) mushrooms, sliced
Cooking time: 15 minutes	**1 teaspoon red or green Thai curry paste**
	150 ml (¼ pint) fish stock
	150 ml (¼ pint) coconut milk
Serves: 1	**100 g (3½ oz) raw tiger prawns, peeled and deveined**
	2 spring onions, sliced
	100 g (3½ oz) cooked rice noodles
	1 tablespoon chopped fresh coriander

Heat the oil in a saucepan, add the red pepper and mushrooms and cook for 3–4 minutes. Add the curry paste and cook, stirring, for 1 minute.

Add the stock and coconut milk and bring to the boil. Reduce the heat and simmer for 5 minutes.

Add the prawns, spring onions, noodles and coriander, stir to mix and cook for 3–4 minutes until the prawns have turned pink and are cooked through.

COOK'S NOTES You can make this recipe with ready-prepared cooked peeled prawns, for added convenience, in which case add them right at the end so that they don't overcook but just heat through.

180 Stir-fried tofu with prawns

Preparation time: 10 minutes, plus marinating	**250 g (8 oz) firm tofu**
	3 tablespoons soy sauce
	1 tablespoon clear honey
	1 tablespoon soya or groundnut oil
Cooking time: 10 minutes	**150 g (5 oz) spring greens, shredded**
	300 g (10 oz) cooked rice noodles
	200 g (7 oz) cooked peeled prawns
Serves: 2	**4 tablespoons hoisin sauce**
	2 tablespoons chopped fresh coriander

Pat the tofu dry with kitchen paper and cut it into 1.5 cm (¾ inch) dice. Mix the soy sauce and honey in a small bowl, then add the tofu and mix gently. Cover and leave to marinate for 10 minutes.

Lift the tofu from the marinade with a fork; drain and reserve the marinade. Pat the tofu dry with kitchen paper. Heat the oil in a wok or large frying pan, add the tofu and stir-fry for 3–5 minutes or until golden all over. Remove with a slotted spoon, drain on kitchen paper and keep warm.

Add the greens to the pan and quickly stir-fry until wilted. Return the tofu to the pan with the noodles and prawns and heat through, tossing the ingredients together, for 2 minutes.

Mix the hoisin sauce with the reserved marinade. Stir into the pan, scatter over the coriander and serve immediately.

COOK'S NOTES Stir-frying is one of the best, and quickest, ways to cook tofu, particularly when it has been marinated in soy sauce for extra flavour. Pre-packed, ready-cooked noodles make a perfect partner, cutting down on cooking time as well as saucepans.

7 Poultry and Game

181 Chicken thighs with fresh pesto

182 Duck with oranges and cranberries

Preparation time:
5 minutes

Cooking time:
25 minutes

Serves: **4**

1 tablespoon olive oil
8 chicken thighs
steamed vegetables, to serve

PESTO
6 tablespoons olive oil
50 g (2 oz) pine nuts, toasted
50 g (2 oz) Parmesan cheese, freshly
** grated**
50 g (2 oz) basil leaves, plus extra to
** garnish**
15 g (½ oz) parsley, roughly chopped
2 garlic cloves, chopped
salt and pepper

Heat the oil in a nonstick frying pan, add the chicken thighs and cook gently, turning frequently, for 20 minutes or until cooked through.

Meanwhile, to make the pesto, put all the ingredients in a blender or food processor and blend until smooth.

Remove the chicken from the pan and keep it hot. Reduce the heat, add the pesto and heat through for 2–3 minutes.

Pour the warmed pesto over the chicken thighs, garnish with basil and serve with steamed vegetables.

Preparation time:
10 minutes

Cooking time:
10–16 minutes

Serves: **4**

Oven temperature:
200°C (400°F) Gas Mark 6

4 duck breasts, about 200 g (7 oz) each
salt and pepper
mashed potatoes, to serve (optional)

SAUCE
2 oranges
50 g (2 oz) cranberries
4 tablespoons soft light brown sugar
1 tablespoon clear honey

Score the skin of each duck breast through to the flesh 4 times and rub generously with salt and pepper. Heat a heavy-based frying pan or ridged griddle pan until hot. Add the duck breasts, skin side down, and cook for 6–10 minutes, then turn over and cook on the other side for a further 4–6 minutes.

Transfer the duck to a roasting tin, skin side down, and roast in a preheated oven, 200°C (400°F), Gas Mark 6, for 5 minutes. Remove from the oven and leave to rest for 3 minutes.

Meanwhile, remove the peel and pith from the oranges. Working over a bowl to catch the juice, cut between the membranes to remove the segments. Put the segments and juice, cranberries and sugar in a saucepan with salt and pepper to taste and simmer until the cranberries are soft. Stir in the honey.

Remove the duck from the pan, cut it into diagonal slices and arrange them on warmed serving plates. Pour over the sauce. Serve with mashed potatoes, if you like.

COOK'S NOTES This quick, cheap dish is great served with fresh vegetables or a spinach salad. If you want to make it even easier, simply buy a jar of high-quality pesto from your usual supermarket. Use a couple of tablespoons per portion.

183 Duck with honey and lime sauce

Preparation time: **10 minutes**	**4 duck breasts, about 200 g (7 oz) each** **3 tablespoons clear honey** **150 ml (¼ pint) white wine**
Cooking time: **10 minutes**	**finely grated rind of 1 lime** **75 ml (3 fl oz) lime juice** **100 ml (3½ fl oz) chicken stock**
Serves: **4**	**1 tablespoon finely chopped fresh root ginger**
Oven temperature: **200°C (400°F) Gas Mark 6**	**½ teaspoon arrowroot** **1 tablespoon water** **salt and pepper** **steamed carrots and mangetout, to serve**

Score the skin of each duck breast through to the flesh 4 times and rub generously with salt and pepper. Heat a heavy-based frying pan or ridged griddle pan until hot. Add the duck breasts, skin side down, and cook for 3 minutes. Drain off all the fat from the pan.

Transfer the duck to a roasting tin, skin side down, and brush with 1 tablespoon of the honey. Roast in a preheated oven, 200°C (400°F), Gas Mark 6, for 5 minutes. Remove from the oven and leave to rest for 3 minutes, then diagonally slice.

Meanwhile, add the wine, lime rind and juice, stock, ginger and remaining honey to the frying pan, bring to the boil and cook for 5 minutes. Blend the arrowroot with the measured water in a cup and add to the sauce. Return to the boil, stirring constantly, and cook until thickened. Spoon the sauce over the duck. Serve immediately with steamed carrots and mangetout.

COOK'S NOTES This makes a dinner party dish that is guaranteed to impress guests every time, and it's so speedy to prepare. Make sure that the duck skin really crisps up without burning before transferring the meat to the oven to finish cooking. The duck should be slightly pink inside.

184 Grilled poussins with citrus glaze

Preparation time: **10 minutes**	**2 poussins, halved, about 750 g (1½ lb) each** **50 g (2 oz) butter, softened**
Cooking time: **about 20 minutes**	**2 tablespoons olive oil** **2 garlic cloves, crushed** **½ teaspoon dried thyme**
Serves: **4**	**¼ teaspoon cayenne pepper** **finely grated rind and juice of 1 lemon** **finely grated rind and juice of 1 lime** **2 tablespoons clear honey** **salt and pepper**

TO SERVE
grilled tomatoes
green salad

Roll the poussin halves with a rolling pin to flatten them slightly. Put the butter in a small bowl and beat in half the oil, the garlic, thyme, cayenne, salt and pepper to taste, half the lemon and lime rind and 1 tablespoon each of the lemon and lime juice.

Carefully loosen the skin of each poussin breast and, using a round-bladed knife, spread the citrus mixture evenly between the skin and breast meat.

Mix together the remaining oil, lemon and lime juice and rind and honey in a small bowl. Put the poussins, skin-side up, on a grill pan and brush with the mixture. Cook under a preheated medium-high grill on one side for 10–12 minutes, basting once or twice with the juices. Turn over and grill on the other side for 7–10 minutes. The bird is cooked once the thigh juices run clear when pierced with a knife.

Serve with grilled tomatoes and a green salad.

COOK'S NOTES Use this recipe for any small game birds, such as quails, pigeons and partridges.

185 Chicken with apple and Calvados

Preparation time:	1 tablespoon olive oil
10 minutes	**4 boneless, skinless chicken breasts, about 150 g (5 oz) each**
Cooking time:	**200 g (7 oz) shallots, halved**
15 minutes	**1 garlic clove, finely chopped**
	1 apple, cored and diced
Serves: **4**	**75 g (3 oz) button mushrooms, sliced**
	4 tablespoons Calvados or brandy
	250 ml (8 fl oz) chicken stock
	1 teaspoon Dijon mustard
	small bunch of thyme, leaves stripped and finely chopped, plus extra to garnish
	salt and pepper

Heat the oil in a ridged frying pan or griddle pan, add the chicken breasts and shallots and cook for 4 minutes until the chicken is browned on the underside.

Turn the chicken over and add the garlic, apple and mushrooms. Cook for 6 minutes until the chicken is cooked through.

Spoon the Calvados or brandy over the chicken and, when bubbling, flame with a match and stand well back. When the flames subside, add the stock, mustard, thyme and salt and pepper to taste and cook for 5 minutes.

Cut each chicken breast into quarters and arrange the slices on a bed of the shallots, apple and mushrooms. Spoon the sauce around and sprinkle with thyme to garnish.

186 Venison with cranberry confit

Preparation time:	25 g (1 oz) butter
10 minutes	**1 tablespoon olive oil**
	4 venison fillets, about 175 g (6 oz) each, cut from the saddle, tied at intervals with fine string
Cooking time:	
15–20 minutes	**2 red onions, diced**
	150 ml (¼ pint) ruby port
Serves: **4**	**2 teaspoons tomato purée**
	200 g (7 oz) frozen cranberries
Oven temperature:	**4 teaspoons clear honey**
200°C (400°F) Gas Mark 6	**salt and pepper**

TO SERVE
mashed potatoes or swede (optional)
steamed asparagus tips

Heat the butter and oil in a large frying pan, add the venison fillets and cook over a high heat, turning frequently, for 5 minutes until browned.

Transfer the venison to a small roasting tin and roast in a preheated oven, 200°C (400°F), Gas Mark 6, for 10–12 minutes for rare to medium or 13–15 minutes for medium to well done.

Meanwhile, add the onions to the frying pan and cook for 5 minutes. Add the port, tomato purée and cranberries, cover and cook for 5 minutes until the cranberries have softened. Stir in the honey and salt and pepper to taste.

Using a slotted spoon, transfer the onion mixture to the centre of 4 serving plates. Thinly slice the venison and arrange in an overlapping line on top of mashed potatoes or swede, if you like. Spoon the pan juices around the edge of the plates and serve with steamed asparagus tips.

COOK'S NOTES Full of gamey flavour, venison fillets are the most prized of all cuts and take just a matter of minutes to cook. Instead of venison, you can use pork fillets, which should be roasted for 15 minutes in the oven.

187 Venison with blackberry sauce

Preparation time:
10 minutes

Cooking time:
10–12 minutes

Serves: **2**

125 g (4 oz) blackberries, defrosted if frozen
150 ml (¼ pint) game or beef stock
2 venison steaks, about 175 g (6 oz) each
40 g (1½ oz) butter
3 tablespoons crème de cassis
salt and pepper
stir-fried green vegetables, to serve

Reserve a quarter of the blackberries and blend the remainder in a blender or food processor with a splash of the stock. Press the purée through a small sieve, preferably non-metallic, into a bowl.

Pat the venison steaks dry with kitchen paper and season generously with salt and pepper.

Heat half the butter in a frying pan until bubbling, add the venison steaks and cook for 3–4 minutes on each side until well browned. Drain and transfer to warmed serving plates.

Add the blackberry purée to the pan with the remaining stock. Bring to the boil and cook until the sauce is thick enough to coat the back of a spoon. Add the cassis and the remaining butter and reserved berries. Heat through, stirring, until the butter has melted and the sauce is rich and glossy. Spoon it over the venison steaks and serve immediately with stir-fried green vegetables.

COOK'S NOTES Tender, succulent fillet or loin steaks are ideal for this dish, although haunch makes a good, if a little firmer, alternative. Fry the steaks for 6 minutes on each side if you prefer them well done. Serve with some stir-fried green vegetables.

188 Oriental duck with roasted squash

Preparation time:
10 minutes

Cooking time:
20 minutes

Serves: **2**

Oven temperature:
220°C (425°F) Gas Mark 7

250 g (8 oz) butternut squash, peeled, deseeded and diced
4 teaspoons olive oil
2 duck breasts, about 200 g (7 oz) each
1 teaspoon Thai seven-spice seasoning
2 star anise
50 g (2 oz) frisée
1 tablespoon chopped chives, plus extra whole chives to garnish
salt and pepper

SMOKE MIX
8 tablespoons jasmine tea leaves
8 tablespoons soft light brown sugar
8 tablespoons white long-grain rice

DRESSING
2.5 cm (1 inch) piece of fresh root ginger, peeled and grated
1 tablespoon rice vinegar
pinch of dried red chilli flakes
4 tablespoons sunflower oil

Toss the squash with 3 teaspoons of the oil in a roasting tin. Season to taste with salt and pepper. Roast in a preheated oven, 220°C (425°F), Gas Mark 7, for 20 minutes.

Meanwhile, mix all the dressing ingredients in a bowl. Brush the duck with the remaining oil and rub with 1 teaspoon salt and the seven-spice seasoning. Line a wok with 1 or 2 sheets of foil, making sure that it touches the base. Add the smoke mix ingredients and star anise and stir together, then place a trivet over the top. Put the duck on the trivet, cover tightly and smoke over medium heat for 12 minutes. Remove from the heat and leave to stand, covered, for 5 minutes.

Put the frisée and chives in a serving bowl, add the squash and dressing and toss to mix. Slice the duck breasts, garnish with whole chives and serve with the vegetables.

189 Duck salad with roasted peaches

190 Venison sausages with spicy bean sauce

Preparation time:	4 peaches, stoned and quartered
10 minutes	1 tablespoon caster sugar
	½ teaspoon ground cinnamon
Cooking time:	4 duck breast fillets, about 250 g (8 oz)
15 minutes	each, skinned
	4 tablespoons extra virgin olive oil
Serves: 4	50 ml (2 fl oz) Marsala
	2 tablespoons balsamic vinegar
Oven temperature:	salt and pepper
220°C (425°F) Gas Mark 7	salad leaves, to serve

Put the peach quarters, cut side up, in a roasting tin. Mix the sugar and cinnamon in a cup and sprinkle evenly over the peaches. Bake in a preheated oven, 220°C (425°F), Gas Mark 7, for 15 minutes or until softened but not collapsed.

Meanwhile, season the duck breasts to taste with salt and pepper. Heat 1 tablespoon of the oil in a frying pan, add the duck and cook for 3–4 minutes on each side. Remove it from the pan, wrap loosely in foil and leave to rest for 5 minutes.

Stir the Marsala and vinegar into the pan, bring to the boil and cook until reduced by half, then strain into a bowl. Whisk in the remaining oil and any juices from the duck, then season to taste with salt and pepper.

Arrange the peach quarters on serving plates. Thinly slice the duck and add to the plates with some salad leaves. Pour over the dressing and serve immediately.

Preparation time:	8 venison sausages
10 minutes	1 tablespoon sunflower oil
	1 onion, chopped
Cooking time:	1 red pepper, cored, deseeded and diced
12 minutes	1 courgette, diced
	2 flat cap mushrooms, sliced
Serves: 4	400 g (13 oz) can red kidney beans,
	drained and rinsed
	400 g (13 oz) can chopped tomatoes
	1 teaspoon chopped red chilli
	1 teaspoon wholegrain mustard
	2 teaspoons brown sugar
	salt and pepper
	crusty bread, to serve

Cook the sausages under a preheated high grill for 10–12 minutes until browned and cooked through.

Meanwhile, heat the oil in a large frying pan, add the onion and cook for 3 minutes. Add the red pepper, courgette and mushrooms and cook for 3 minutes. Stir in the remaining ingredients and bring to the boil. Reduce the heat, cover and simmer for 5 minutes until thickened.

Spoon the bean mixture into warmed serving bowls and serve with the sausages and crusty bread.

COOK'S NOTES Marsala is a Sicilian fortified wine with an intense, sweet herb flavour. It is available from supermarkets and wine shops, but you could use port instead. To remove the duck skin, simply hold the breast fillet at one end and pull the skin away from the meat. You may need to use a sharp knife to help ease the skin away from the flesh.

191 Blue cheese and chicken wraps

192 Chicken and goats' cheese burger

Preparation time:
10 minutes

Cooking time:
18–20 minutes

Serves: **4**

Oven temperature:
190°C (375°F) Gas Mark 5

**4 boneless, skinless chicken breasts,
   about 150 g (5 oz) each**
125 g (4 oz) Gorgonzola cheese, quartered
4 sun-dried tomatoes in oil, drained
**4 slices of Serrano ham, about 50 g (2 oz)
   in total**
2 tablespoons olive oil
salt and pepper

TO SERVE
griddled asparagus
griddled tomatoes on the vine

Using a sharp knife, make a horizontal slit in each chicken breast. Do not cut all the way through but just deep enough to create a pocket in the flesh. Tuck a piece of Gorgonzola and a sun-dried tomato into each pocket, season to taste with salt and pepper, then wrap each breast in a slice of ham.

Lay the chicken breasts, the join in the ham downwards, on a foil-lined baking sheet. Drizzle with the oil, then cook in a preheated oven, 190°C (375°F), Gas Mark 5, for 18–20 minutes until the ham has darkened and the chicken is cooked through. Transfer to individual plates and serve with griddled asparagus and tomatoes.

COOK'S NOTES These wraps can be prepared ahead of time and popped in the oven just before you are ready to eat. For a slightly milder tasting dish, use brie, Camembert or Cheddar instead of Gorgonzola.

Preparation time:
10 minutes

Cooking time:
20 minutes

Serves: **4**

Oven temperature:
200°C (400°F) Gas Mark 6

**500 g (1 lb) cooked chicken breast,
   thickly sliced**
2 tablespoons chopped thyme
2 garlic cloves, crushed
4 thin slices of Parma ham
150 g (5 oz) goats' cheese, sliced
salt and pepper

HONEY-ROASTED FIGS
6 figs, quartered
**2 tablespoons olive oil, plus extra for
   brushing**
**2 tablespoons clear orange blossom
   honey**
salt and pepper

TO SERVE
4 crusty rolls
75 g (3 oz) rocket leaves

Put the figs in an ovenproof dish and drizzle with the oil and honey. Season well with salt and pepper and roast in a preheated oven, 200°C (400°F), Gas Mark 6, for 10 minutes until the figs just start to colour.

Meanwhile, lay the chicken breasts between 2 sheets of clingfilm or nonstick baking paper and flatten slightly with a rolling pin or meat mallet. Rub the thyme and garlic into the chicken, season to taste with salt and pepper and wrap with the ham.

Heat a ridged griddle pan until smoking. Brush the chicken with oil, then add to the pan, reduce the heat to medium and cook for 8 minutes on each side or until cooked through. Top each breast with a slice of goats' cheese and melt slightly under a preheated high grill.

Halve the rolls horizontally and toast under the grill. Top each base with rocket leaves and a chicken breast. Spoon the figs over each burger and serve with the lids on the side with extra rocket leaves.

193 Peppered chicken skewers with rosemary

194 Chicken fajitas

Preparation time:
**10 minutes, plus
marinating**

Cooking time:
8–10 minutes

Serves: **4**

**4 boneless, skinless chicken breasts,
    about 150 g (5 oz) each
2 tablespoons finely chopped rosemary
2 garlic cloves, finely chopped
3 tablespoons lemon juice
2 teaspoons prepared English mustard
1 tablespoon clear honey
2 teaspoons pepper
1 tablespoon olive oil
salt
salad, to serve (optional)**

Lay the chicken breasts between 2 sheets of clingfilm or nonstick baking paper and flatten slightly with a rolling pin or meat mallet. Cut the chicken into thick strips.

Put the chicken in a large, shallow bowl. Add all the remaining ingredients and mix well. Cover and leave to marinate in a cool place for 5–10 minutes.

Thread the chicken strips on to 8 metal skewers and cook under a preheated grill on its highest setting for 4–5 minutes on each side or until the chicken is cooked through. Serve immediately with a salad, such as baby spinach leaves with red onion, if you like.

Preparation time:
15 minutes

Cooking time:
10 minutes

Serves: **4**

**1 tablespoon olive oil
1 large red onion, thinly sliced
1 red pepper, cored, deseeded and thinly
    sliced
1 yellow pepper, cored, deseeded and
    thinly sliced
450 g (14½ oz) boneless, skinless chicken
    breasts, sliced into thin strips
⅛ teaspoon paprika
⅛ teaspoon mild chilli powder
⅛ teaspoon ground cumin
¼ teaspoon dried oregano
4 soft flour tortillas
½ iceberg lettuce, finely shredded
guacamole, to serve (optional)**

TOMATO SALSA
**1 small red onion, finely chopped
425 g (14 oz) small vine-ripened tomatoes
2 garlic cloves, crushed
large handful of fresh coriander leaves,
    chopped
pepper**

To make the salsa, mix all the ingredients together in a bowl and season to taste with pepper.

Heat the oil in a wok or large, nonstick frying pan, add the onion and peppers and stir-fry for 3–4 minutes. Add the chicken, paprika, chilli powder, cumin and oregano and stir-fry for 5 minutes or until the chicken is cooked through.

Meanwhile, wrap the tortillas in foil and warm in the oven for 5 minutes, or according to the packet instructions

Spoon a quarter of the chicken mixture into the centre of each tortilla, add a couple of tablespoons of the salsa and the lettuce and roll up. Serve immediately, accompanied by guacamole, if you like.

195 Chicken teriyaki

Preparation time:
10 minutes

Cooking time:
10 minutes

Serves: **4**

**750 g (1½ lb) boneless, skinless chicken
  breasts, cubed**
**12 spring onions, cut into 5 cm (2 inch)
  lengths**
**2 red peppers, cored, deseeded and cut
  into chunks**
2 tablespoons vegetable oil
boiled rice, to serve

SAUCE
3 tablespoons dark soy sauce
3 tablespoons clear honey
3 tablespoons sake or dry sherry
1 garlic clove, crushed
3 slices of peeled fresh root ginger

Put all the sauce ingredients in a small saucepan and simmer for
5 minutes until thickened.

Meanwhile, divide the chicken cubes, spring onions and red peppers
among 8 metal skewers and brush with oil.

Heat a ridged griddle pan until hot. Add the chicken skewers and cook
for 4 minutes on each side or until cooked through. Alternatively, cook
under a preheated high grill.

Brush the skewers with the teriyaki sauce and serve on a bed of boiled
rice, drizzled with more sauce.

COOK'S NOTES Sake is widely used in Japanese cooking and adds
a really authentic flavour, but if you don't have any to hand, you can use
dry sherry instead. Try to use Japanese-brewed soy sauce rather than
Chinese soy sauce, which has a saltier, less malty taste. You can use
bamboo skewers instead of metal ones, but they need to be presoaked in
cold water for 30 minutes.

196 Lemon grass chicken with vegetables

Preparation time:
15 minutes

Cooking time:
5–10 minutes

Serves: **4**

18 lemon grass stalks
8 boneless, skinless chicken thighs
1 garlic clove
2 kaffir lime leaves, torn into pieces
2 tablespoons soy sauce
1 teaspoon sesame oil
1 red pepper, cored, deseeded and sliced
**1 green pepper, cored, deseeded and
  sliced**
350 g (12 oz) sugar snap peas
2 pak choi, quartered lengthways

Chop 2 of the lemon grass stalks. Put the chicken, chopped lemon grass,
garlic, lime leaves and half the soy sauce in a food processor and
process until well combined.

Divide the mixture into 16 portions, then mould each portion around a
lemon grass stalk 'skewer', forming it into a sausage shape.

Put on a baking sheet, drizzle with half the oil and cook under a
preheated high grill for 4–5 minutes, turning occasionally, until golden
and cooked through (you may need to cook the skewers in 2 batches).

Meanwhile, heat the remaining oil in a wok or large frying pan, add the
vegetables and stir-fry for 2–3 minutes until just tender, then add the
remaining soy sauce. Serve the stir-fried vegetables with the chicken.

COOK'S NOTES If you have time, presoak the lemon grass stalks in
cold water for 30 minutes to prevent them from burning under the grill.

197 Chicken with pak choi and ginger

198 Chargrilled chicken with coriander salsa

Preparation time:
10 minutes, plus marinating

Cooking time:
about 20 minutes

Serves: **2**

1 cm (½ inch) piece of fresh root ginger, peeled and grated
1 small garlic clove, crushed
1 tablespoon dark soy sauce
1 tablespoon tangerine syrup
1½ teaspoons mirin (Japanese rice wine)
1 teaspoon sugar
pinch of Chinese five-spice powder
2 boneless, skinless chicken breasts, about 150 g (5 oz) each
2 pak choi, halved
fresh coriander sprigs, to garnish

GINGER SALSA
2.5 cm (1 inch) piece of fresh root ginger, peeled and very finely shredded
1 red chilli, deseeded and finely chopped
a few fresh coriander leaves, chopped
1 teaspoon sesame oil
juice of ½ lime
salt and pepper

Mix together the ginger, garlic, soy sauce, tangerine syrup, mirin, sugar and five-spice powder in a bowl. Put the chicken in a shallow, heatproof dish, pour over the mixture and turn to coat thoroughly. Cover and leave to marinate in a cool place for 5–10 minutes.

Meanwhile, to make the ginger salsa, mix all the ingredients together in a small bowl and season to taste with salt and pepper.

Put the chicken with the marinade in a bamboo steamer and steam for 8 minutes. Remove the chicken and keep warm. Steam the pak choi in the cooking juices for 2–3 minutes. Serve the chicken and pak choi with the salsa, garnished with coriander sprigs.

Preparation time:
10 minutes, plus marinating

Cooking time:
16 minutes

Serves: **4**

2 tablespoons dark soy sauce
2 teaspoons sesame oil
1 tablespoon olive oil
2 teaspoons clear honey
pinch of dried red chilli flakes
4 large boneless, skinless chicken breasts, about 200 g (7 oz) each
diced tomato and steamed couscous, to serve

CORIANDER SALSA
1 red onion, diced
1 small garlic clove, crushed
1 bunch of fresh coriander, roughly chopped
6 tablespoons extra virgin olive oil
finely grated rind and juice of 1 lemon
1 teaspoon ground cumin
salt and pepper

Mix the soy sauce, oils, honey and chilli flakes together in a shallow dish. Add the chicken and turn to coat thoroughly. Cover and leave to marinate in a cool place for 10 minutes.

Heat a ridged griddle pan until smoking. Lift the chicken from the marinade, drain and reserve the marinade. Add the chicken to the pan, reduce the heat to medium and cook for 8 minutes on each side until charred and cooked through. Remove from the pan, wrap loosely in foil and leave to rest for 5 minutes.

Meanwhile, pour the marinade juices into a small saucepan, bring to the boil and boil vigorously for 2 minutes, then remove from the heat but keep warm. Mix all the salsa ingredients together in a bowl and season to taste with salt and pepper.

Serve the chicken with couscous tossed with diced tomato, and top with the salsa and the marinade sauce.

199 Duck with cinnamon and redcurrant sauce

Preparation time:
10 minutes

Cooking time:
20 minutes

Serves: 2

Oven temperature:
200°C (400°F) Gas Mark 6

2 duck breasts, about 300 g (10 oz) each
1 tablespoon olive oil
1 small red onion, finely chopped
1 garlic clove, finely chopped
200 ml (7 fl oz) chicken stock
200 ml (7 fl oz) red wine
pinch of ground cinnamon
1 tablespoon redcurrant jelly
salt and pepper
Puy lentils and sugar snap peas, to serve
   (optional)

Score the skin of each duck breast through to the flesh 4 times and rub generously with salt and pepper. Heat a heavy-based frying pan or ridged griddle pan until hot. Add the duck breasts, skin side down, and cook for 2–3 minutes. Turn over and brown the other side.

Transfer the duck to a roasting tin and roast in a preheated oven, 200°C (400°F), Gas Mark 6, for 15 minutes or until cooked through.

Meanwhile, heat the oil in a nonstick frying pan, add the onion and garlic and cook for 2–3 minutes. Add the stock, wine and cinnamon and bring to the boil. Leave the sauce to bubble for 10 minutes or until reduced by half. Strain the sauce and discard the onion. Season to taste with pepper and stir in the redcurrant jelly.

Thickly slice the duck and transfer to 2 warmed plates. Spoon over a little of the sauce and serve with Puy lentils and sugar snap peas, if you like.

COOK'S NOTES Duck and redcurrant is a classic combination, with the tart flavour of the berries complementing the rich duck meat. Use real chicken stock for the sauce and a good red wine, as this will make all the difference.

200 Thai chicken with cashews

Preparation time:
10 minutes

Cooking time:
8 minutes

Serves: 4

2 tablespoons vegetable oil
750 g (1½ lb) boneless, skinless chicken
   breasts, thinly sliced
4 garlic cloves, crushed
2 large green chillies, deseeded and
   chopped
1 onion, cut into chunks
1 green pepper, cored, deseeded and cut
   into chunks
5 tablespoons Thai fish sauce
2 tablespoons dark soy sauce
2 tablespoons soft light brown sugar

TO SERVE
25 g (1 oz) cashew nuts, toasted
15 g (½ oz) Thai basil or fresh coriander
   leaves
boiled rice

Heat the oil in a wok or large frying pan until smoking. Add the chicken, garlic and chillies and stir-fry for 1 minute. Add the onion and green pepper and stir-fry for a further 5 minutes until the chicken is cooked through.

Add the fish sauce, soy sauce and sugar and mix well. Bring to the boil, then transfer to a warmed serving dish. Scatter with the cashew nuts and basil or coriander, and serve with boiled rice.

COOK'S NOTES To make this simple Thai stir-fry, look out for Thai sweet, or holy, basil leaves, which have a slightly spicy aniseed flavour. If you can't find them, you can use fresh coriander leaves instead.

8 Meat

201 Lamb cutlets with anchovies

202 Meatballs with fresh tomato sauce

Preparation time:
10 minutes, plus marinating

Cooking time:
10 minutes

Serves: **4**

finely grated rind and juice of ½ lemon
2 garlic cloves, crushed
2 tablespoons extra virgin olive oil, plus extra for brushing
4 rosemary sprigs, finely chopped
4 anchovy fillets in oil, drained and finely chopped
2 tablespoons lemon cordial
12 lamb cutlets, about 40 g (1½ oz) each
salt and pepper

TO SERVE
rocket leaves
sweet potato skins (optional – see Cook's Notes)

Mix together the lemon rind and juice, garlic, oil, rosemary, anchovies and lemon cordial in a bowl. Add the lamb cutlets, season to taste with salt and pepper and turn to coat thoroughly. Cover and leave to marinate in a cool place for 10 minutes.

Cook the lamb cutlets under a preheated high grill for 3–5 minutes on each side or until charred and cooked through. Remove from the heat, keep warm and leave to rest for 5 minutes. Serve the cutlets with rocket leaves and sweet potato skins, if you like.

Preparation time:
10 minutes

Cooking time:
8–10 minutes

Serves: **1**

125 g (4 oz) lean minced pork
1 teaspoon pesto
pinch of dried red chilli flakes
a little beaten egg
75 g (3 oz) dried pasta, such as fusilli or rigatoni
1 teaspoon olive oil
100 g (3½ oz) cherry tomatoes, halved
handful of basil, torn
salt and pepper

Mix together the minced pork, pesto, chilli flakes and salt and pepper to taste in a bowl. Mix in enough beaten egg to bind the mixture.

Bring a large saucepan of water to the boil. Add the pasta, return to the boil and cook for 8–10 minutes, or according to the packet instructions, until tender but still firm to the bite.

Meanwhile, heat the oil in a nonstick frying pan. Shape the meat mixture into 8 small, evenly sized balls. Add the meatballs to the pan and cook for 4–5 minutes until browned all over and cooked through.

Drain the pasta thoroughly. Toss with the tomatoes, basil and meatballs and serve immediately.

COOK'S NOTES These lamb cutlets are delicious served with sweet potato skins, which are easy to make. Simply bake 4 sweet potatoes in their skins in a preheated oven, 200°C (400°F), Gas Mark 6, for about 45–60 minutes, depending on size, until soft. Quarter, scoop out some of the flesh and brush the skins with oil. Season to taste with salt and pepper and cook under a preheated high grill until crisp.

203 Cheesy pork with parsnip purée

Preparation time:
10 minutes

Cooking time:
20 minutes

Serves: **4**

Oven temperature:
200°C (400°F) Gas Mark 6

**4 lean pork steaks, about 125 g (4 oz)
    each
1 teaspoon olive oil
50 g (2 oz) crumbly cheese, such as
    Wensleydale or Cheshire, crumbled
½ tablespoon chopped sage
75 g (3 oz) fresh granary breadcrumbs
1 egg yolk, beaten
steamed green beans or cabbage, to
    serve**

PARSNIP PURÉE
**625 g (1¼ lb) parsnips, chopped
2 garlic cloves
3 tablespoons crème fraîche
pepper**

Season the pork steaks with plenty of pepper. Heat the oil in a nonstick frying pan, add the pork steaks and cook for 2 minutes on each side until browned, then transfer to an ovenproof dish.

Mix together the cheese, sage, breadcrumbs and egg yolk in a bowl. Divide the mixture into 4 and use it to top each of the pork steaks, pressing down gently. Cook in a preheated oven, 200°C (400°F), Gas Mark 6, for 12–15 minutes until the topping is golden.

Meanwhile, bring a large saucepan of water to the boil, add the parsnips and garlic and cook for 10–12 minutes until tender. Drain and mash with the crème fraîche and plenty of pepper, then serve with the pork steaks and some steamed green beans or cabbage.

COOK'S NOTES This is a quick and nutritious recipe that is ideal for a family meal. The cheesy breadcrumb topping would also work well on cod or salmon steaks – just substitute chopped parsley for the sage.

204 Calves' liver with leeks and beans

Preparation time:
10 minutes

Cooking time:
10 minutes

Serves: **1**

**1 piece of calves' liver, about 125 g (4 oz)
1 tablespoon seasoned flour
1 teaspoon olive oil
4 baby leeks or 1 large leek, sliced
1 rasher of lean back bacon, chopped
125 g (4 oz) can cannellini beans, drained
    and rinsed
1 tablespoon crème fraîche
pepper
1 tablespoon chopped parsley or thyme,
    to garnish
green salad, to serve**

Lightly coat the liver in the seasoned flour. Heat half the oil in a nonstick frying pan, add the liver and cook for 2 minutes on each side or until cooked to your liking. Remove from the pan to a warmed serving plate and keep warm in a low oven.

Heat the remaining oil in the frying pan, add the leeks and bacon and cook for 3–4 minutes.

Stir in the beans and crème fraîche, season to taste with pepper and heat through. Serve with the liver, garnished with the parsley or thyme, accompanied by a green salad.

205 Lamb with hummus and tortillas

206 Minty lamb kebabs

Preparation time:
10 minutes, plus marinating

Cooking time:
5–10 minutes

Serves: **4**

500 g (1 lb) fillet of lamb, cut into 1.5 cm (¾ inch) thick slices
finely grated rind and juice of 1 lemon
1 rosemary sprig, chopped
3 mixed peppers, cored, deseeded and chopped
1 small aubergine, sliced
4 soft flour tortillas
rocket leaves, to serve

HUMMUS
400 g (13 oz) can chickpeas, drained and rinsed
2 tablespoons Greek yogurt
2 tablespoons lemon juice
1 tablespoon chopped parsley

Put the lamb, lemon rind and juice, rosemary and peppers in a non-metallic bowl and stir well. Cover and leave to marinate in a cool place for 10 minutes.

Heat a large, heavy-based frying pan or ridged griddle pan until smoking. Add the lamb and pepper mixture and the aubergine and cook, turning once or twice, for 3–4 minutes until the lamb is cooked through (you may need to do this in 2 batches).

Meanwhile, put all the hummus ingredients in a blender or food processor and blend for 30 seconds, then spoon into a bowl. Wrap the tortillas in foil and warm in the oven for 5 minutes, or according to the packet instructions.

When the lamb and vegetables are cooked, wrap in the tortillas with the hummus and serve with rocket leaves.

Preparation time:
10 minutes, plus marinating

Cooking time:
8–10 minutes

Serves: **4**

1 garlic clove, crushed
2 tablespoons chopped mint
1 tablespoon mint sauce
150 ml (¼ pint) low-fat natural yogurt
350 g (12 oz) lean lamb, cubed
2 small onions, cut into wedges
1 green pepper, cored, deseeded and cut into wedges

TO SERVE
green salad
couscous
lemon wedges (optional)

Mix together the garlic, mint, mint sauce and yogurt in a bowl. Add the lamb and stir well. Cover and leave to marinate in a cool place for 10 minutes.

Thread the lamb and onion and pepper wedges on to 8 metal skewers and cook under a preheated high grill for 8–10 minutes until cooked through.

Serve immediately with green salad, couscous and lemon wedges, if you like.

COOK'S NOTES If you have more time, allow the lamb to marinate for an hour in the fridge to absorb more of the flavours. The kebabs can be cooked on the barbecue in summer. The metal skewers help to cook the meat through, but always check it's thoroughly cooked before serving.

207 Lamb cutlets with herb crust

208 Peppered lamb with yogurt dressing

Preparation time: **10 minutes**	**12 lean lamb cutlets**, about 40 g (1½ oz) each
	2 tablespoons pesto
Cooking time: **15 minutes**	**3 tablespoons fresh granary breadcrumbs**
	1 tablespoon chopped walnuts, toasted
	1 teaspoon olive oil
Serves: **4**	**2 garlic cloves, crushed**
	625 g (1¼ lb) greens, finely shredded and blanched
Oven temperature: **200°C (400°F) Gas Mark 6**	
	TO SERVE
	baby carrots
	cabbage

Heat a large nonstick frying pan or ridged griddle pan until smoking. Add the lamb cutlets and cook for 1 minute on each side, then transfer them to a baking sheet.

Mix together the pesto, breadcrumbs and walnuts in a small bowl and use to top each of the cutlets, pressing down gently. Cook in a preheated oven, 200°C (400°F), Gas Mark 6, for 10–12 minutes.

Meanwhile, heat the oil in a wok or large frying pan, add the garlic and stir-fry for 1 minute, then add the greens and stir-fry for 3–4 minutes until tender.

Serve the stir-fried greens with the lamb, accompanied by baby carrots and cabbage.

Preparation time: **10 minutes**	**2 teaspoons pepper**
	2 teaspoons salt
	2 teaspoons ground cumin
Cooking time: **6–8 minutes**	**2 lamb loin fillets**, about 250 g (8 oz) each
	extra virgin olive oil, for brushing
	75 g (3 oz) watercress
Serves: **4**	**250 g (8 oz) cooked beetroot in natural juices**, drained and chopped

MINT YOGURT
125 ml (4 fl oz) Greek yogurt
1 tablespoon chopped mint

DRESSING
1 tablespoon walnut oil
1 teaspoon white wine vinegar
salt and pepper

Mix together the pepper, salt and cumin on a plate. Brush the lamb loins with oil, then press into the spice mixture to coat evenly.

Heat a heavy-based frying pan until hot. Add the lamb loins and cook for 3–4 minutes on each side. Remove them from the pan, wrap loosely in foil and leave to rest for 5 minutes.

Meanwhile, mix together the yogurt and mint in a small bowl and season to taste with salt and pepper. Mix together the watercress and beetroot in a large bowl. Whisk together the dressing ingredients in another small bowl and season to taste with salt and pepper, add to the salad ingredients and toss to coat evenly. Slice the lamb and serve with the salad and the yogurt dressing.

COOK'S NOTES The meat used in this dish comes from the eye fillet, or tenderloin, which runs along the back of the lamb and is particularly sweet and tender.

209 Gammon steaks with creamy lentils

210 Chorizo and chickpea stew

Preparation time:
5 minutes

Cooking time:
25 minutes

Serves: **4**

125 g (4 oz) Puy lentils
50 g (2 oz) butter
2 shallots, peeled but left whole
1 garlic clove, chopped
**2 thyme sprigs, crushed, plus extra
  leaves to garnish**
1 teaspoon cumin seeds
4 teaspoons Dijon mustard
2 teaspoons clear honey
4 gammon steaks, about 175 g (6 oz) each
125 ml (4 fl oz) dry cider
75 ml (3 fl oz) single cream
salt and pepper

Preparation time:
5 minutes

Cooking time:
25 minutes

Serves: **4**

500 g (1 lb) new potatoes
1 teaspoon olive oil
2 red onions, chopped
**2 red peppers, cored, deseeded and
  chopped**
**100 g (3½ oz) chorizo sausage, thinly
  sliced**
**500 g (1 lb) plum tomatoes, chopped, or a
  400 g (13 oz) can tomatoes, drained**
**400 g (13 oz) can chickpeas, drained and
  rinsed**
2 tablespoons chopped parsley
crusty bread, to serve

Put the lentils in a saucepan and cover with cold water. Bring to the boil, then reduce the heat and simmer for 20 minutes.

Meanwhile, heat the butter in a frying pan, add the shallots, garlic, thyme and cumin and cook for 10 minutes until the shallots are soft and golden.

Blend the mustard and honey together in a cup and season to taste with salt and pepper. Brush the mixture over the gammon steaks. Cook under a preheated high grill for 3 minutes on each side until golden and cooked through. Keep warm.

Drain the lentils and add to the shallot mixture. Add the cider, bring to the boil and cook until reduced to about 4 tablespoons. Stir in the cream, heat through briefly and season to taste with salt and pepper. Serve with the gammon steaks, garnished with thyme leaves.

Bring a saucepan of water to the boil. Add the potatoes and cook for 12–15 minutes until tender. Drain, then slice.

Meanwhile, heat the oil in a large frying pan, add the onions and red peppers and cook for 3–4 minutes. Add the chorizo and cook for 2 minutes.

Add the potato slices, tomatoes and chickpeas and bring to the boil. Reduce the heat and simmer for 10 minutes. Scatter over the parsley and serve with some crusty bread to mop up all the juices.

COOK'S NOTES This chunky stew is based on hearty rustic Italian recipes. The chorizo sausage provides a wonderfully rich flavour, while the chickpeas make it a filling meal. Use fresh crusty bread to mop up the delicious juices.

211 Roast pork with rosemary and fennel

212 Polenta pork with parsnip mash

Preparation time:	
5 minutes	**1 large rosemary sprig, plus extra sprigs to garnish**
	3 garlic cloves, peeled
Cooking time:	**750 g (1½ lb) pork fillet**
25 minutes	**4 tablespoons olive oil**
	2 fennel bulbs, trimmed and cut into
Serves: **4**	**wedges, central core removed**
	150 ml (¼ pint) white wine
Oven temperature:	**75 g (3 oz) mascarpone cheese**
230°C (450°F) Gas Mark 8	**salt and pepper**

Break the rosemary sprig into short lengths and cut the garlic into slices. Pierce the pork with a sharp knife and insert the pieces of rosemary and garlic evenly all over the fillet. Heat half the oil in a frying pan, add the pork and cook for 5 minutes or until browned all over.

Lightly brush a roasting tin with some of the remaining oil, add the fennel and drizzle with the remaining oil. Put the pork on top and season well with salt and pepper. Roast in a preheated oven, 230°C (450°F), Gas Mark 8, for 20 minutes.

Meanwhile, pour the wine into the frying pan, bring to the boil and cook until reduced by half. Stir in the mascarpone and salt and pepper to taste.

Cut the pork into slices and arrange on a warmed serving dish with the fennel. Pour the sauce into the roasting tin and stir with a wooden spatula to scrape up any sediment from the tin, then spoon over the pork and fennel. Serve immediately, garnished with rosemary sprigs.

Preparation time:	
10 minutes	**1 small lean boneless pork chop, about 125 g (4 oz)**
	1 teaspoon seasoned flour
Cooking time:	**a little beaten egg**
15 minutes	**2 tablespoons quick-cooking polenta**
	1 tablespoon freshly grated Parmesan cheese
Serves: **1**	**1 teaspoon vegetable oil**
	2 parsnips, chopped
	1 garlic clove, peeled but left whole
	1 teaspoon chopped thyme
	15 g (½ oz) butter or margarine
	pepper
	lemon wedges, to garnish
	Savoy cabbage, to serve

Lightly coat the pork chop in the seasoned flour, then dip in the beaten egg. Mix the polenta and Parmesan together on a plate, then press the chop into the mixture to evenly coat.

Heat the oil in a nonstick frying pan, add the chop and cook for 5–6 minutes on each side or until cooked through. Remove from the pan to a warmed serving plate and keep warm.

Meanwhile, bring a saucepan of water to the boil, add the parsnips and garlic and cook for 12–15 minutes. Drain and mash with the thyme and butter or margarine, then season well with pepper.

Serve the chop with the parsnip mash and Savoy cabbage, garnished with lemon wedges.

COOK'S NOTES Try preparing this recipe for a quick and delicious Sunday lunch. The meat is infused with the rosemary and garlic and the sauce makes a lovely alternative to the traditional gravy.

213 Lamb with tangy butter beans

214 Lamb noisettes with leeks

Preparation time:
10 minutes

Cooking time:
10 minutes

Serves: **4**

2 tablespoons finely chopped mint
1 tablespoon finely chopped thyme
1 tablespoon finely chopped oregano
½ tablespoon finely chopped rosemary
4 teaspoons wholegrain mustard
4 lamb noisettes, about 125 g (4 oz) each
mixed salad leaves, to serve (optional)

TANGY BUTTER BEANS
2 teaspoons vegetable oil
1 onion, chopped
1 tablespoon tomato purée
50 ml (2 fl oz) pineapple juice
2 tablespoons lemon juice
a few drops of Tabasco sauce
250 g (8 oz) drained canned butter beans
pepper

Mix together all the chopped herbs on a plate. Spread mustard on both sides of each noisette, then press into the herb mixture to coat evenly.

To make the tangy butter beans, heat the oil in a frying pan, add the onion and cook for 5 minutes. Add the remaining ingredients to the pan and cook gently for 5 minutes.

Meanwhile, cook the lamb noisettes under a preheated high grill for 4 minutes on each side or until cooked but still slightly pink in the centre.

Serve the lamb immediately, surrounded by the tangy butter beans and accompanied by mixed salad leaves, if you like.

Preparation time:
10 minutes

Cooking time:
10 minutes

Serves: **4**

8 loin lamb chops
3 tablespoons redcurrant jelly
1 tablespoon olive oil
25 g (1 oz) butter
2 leeks, thinly sliced
1 tablespoon capers, drained and rinsed
small handful of rosemary or mint leaves, chopped, plus extra to garnish
2 teaspoons pink peppercorns in brine, drained and rinsed
salt and pepper

Roll up the lamb chops tightly and secure each with 2 cocktail sticks. Put the chops on a foil-lined grill pan, dot with the redcurrant jelly and season to taste with salt and pepper.

Cook under a preheated high grill for 5 minutes. Turn them over, spoon the redcurrant jelly juices over the lamb and cook for a further 5 minutes.

Meanwhile, heat the oil and butter in a frying pan, add the leeks, capers, herbs and peppercorns and cook for 5 minutes until softened and just beginning to brown. Spoon on to warmed serving plates. Arrange the lamb on top of the leek mixture, remove the cocktail sticks and serve, sprinkled with extra herbs to garnish.

COOK'S NOTES This elegant yet effortless dish is the perfect choice for special-occasion entertaining.

215 Pork medallions with figs

216 Pork fillet with pesto

Preparation time: **10 minutes**	**2 tablespoons olive oil** **8 pork medallions, about 675 g (1 lb 6 oz)** **in total**
Cooking time: **15 minutes**	**2 onions, thinly sliced** **2 garlic cloves, crushed** **150 g (5 oz) ready-to-eat dried figs,** **thickly sliced**
Serves: **4**	**125 ml (4 fl oz) cream sherry or Marsala** **300 ml (½ pint) chicken stock** **3 teaspoons thick-set honey** **2 tablespoons crème fraîche** **salt and pepper** **torn flat leaf parsley leaves and paprika,** **to garnish** **buttered soft polenta, to serve**

Heat the oil in a large frying pan over a high heat, add the pork medallions and cook until browned on one side. Turn the pork over, add the onions and garlic and cook, turning the pork once or twice and stirring the onions, for 5 minutes until both are browned.

Add the figs, sherry or Marsala, stock, honey and salt and pepper to taste and cook over a medium heat for 5 minutes until the sauce has reduced and the pork is thoroughly cooked. Stir in the crème fraîche.

Garnish with torn parsley leaves and a little paprika, and serve on a bed of soft polenta.

Preparation time: **10 minutes**	**2 pork tenderloin fillets, about 400 g** **(13 oz) each** **6 tablespoons extra virgin olive oil**
Cooking time: **20 minutes**	**50 g (2 oz) blanched almonds** **1 garlic clove, crushed** **1 bunch of flat leaf parsley**
Serves: **4**	**2 tablespoons freshly grated Parmesan** **cheese**
Oven temperature: **190°C (375°F) Gas Mark 5**	**salt and pepper**
	TO SERVE **boiled new potatoes** **green salad**

Trim any gristle from the pork fillets, cut in half crossways and season to taste with salt and pepper. Heat 1 tablespoon of the oil in a frying pan, add the meat and cook for 2–3 minutes until browned all over. Transfer to a roasting dish and cook in a preheated oven, 190°C (375°F), Gas Mark 5, for 15 minutes until cooked through. Remove from the oven, wrap loosely in foil and leave to rest for 5 minutes.

Meanwhile, heat a nonstick frying pan, add the almonds and cook, stirring, until lightly browned. Remove from the pan and leave to cool slightly. Transfer to a food processor with the garlic, parsley, remaining oil and salt and pepper to taste. Process to form a fairly smooth paste. Stir in the Parmesan and taste and adjust the seasoning, if necessary.

Slice the pork, arrange on warmed serving plates with any pan juices and serve with boiled new potatoes and salad, drizzled with spoonfuls of the pesto.

217 Lambs' liver with cranberries

218 Red-hot hamburgers

Preparation time:
10 minutes

Cooking time:
15 minutes

Serves: **4**

2 tablespoons olive oil
2 onions, thinly sliced
150 g (5 oz) smoked back bacon, diced
25 g (1 oz) butter
625 g (1¼ lb) lambs' liver, sliced
2 tablespoons cranberry sauce
2 tablespoons red wine vinegar
75 g (3 oz) frozen cranberries
2 tablespoons water
salt and pepper
mashed potatoes, to serve

Preparation time:
10 minutes

Cooking time:
8–16 minutes

Serves: **4**

600 g (1 lb 3 oz) minced beef
2 garlic cloves, crushed
1 red onion, finely chopped
1 red chilli, finely chopped
1 bunch of parsley, chopped
1 tablespoon Worcestershire sauce
1 egg, beaten
4 baps or wholegrain hamburger buns,
  split
spicy salad leaves, such as rocket or
  mizuna
1 beef tomato, sliced
salt and pepper
relish, to serve

Heat the oil in a large frying pan, add the onions and bacon and cook over a medium heat, stirring occasionally, for 10 minutes until deep golden brown. Remove from the pan and set aside.

Heat the butter in the pan, add the liver slices and cook over a high heat, turning once or twice, for 3 minutes until browned on the outside and just pink in the centre.

Add the cranberry sauce, vinegar, cranberries and measured water. Season to taste with salt and pepper and cook, stirring, for 2 minutes until the cranberry sauce has melted and the cranberries are heated through and soft. Stir in the fried onions and bacon, then serve with mashed potatoes.

Put the mince in a large bowl, add the garlic, onion, chilli, parsley, Worcestershire sauce, egg and a little salt and pepper and mix well.

Heat a ridged griddle pan until smoking. Divide the meat mixture into 4 and shape into burgers. Add the burgers to the pan and cook for 3 minutes on each side for rare, 5 minutes on each side for medium or 7 minutes on each side for well done. Remove from the pan, keep warm and leave to rest while you griddle the baps or buns.

Wash and dry the pan, then reheat, add the baps or bun halves and cook briefly on each side until lightly charred. Fill each bun with some salad leaves, tomato slices and a burger. Serve immediately with the relish of your choice.

COOK'S NOTES Lambs' liver takes only the briefest time to cook and has a wonderful flavour and succulent texture.

219 Quick-fried veal

Preparation time:
10 minutes

Cooking time:
5–8 minutes

Serves: **4**

4 veal escalopes, about 150 g (5 oz) each
3 tablespoons plain flour
½ tablespoon paprika
3 tablespoons extra virgin olive oil
2 lemons
100 g (3½ oz) pitted queen green olives,
** sliced**
3–4 tablespoons chopped chervil, plus
** extra to garnish**
salt and pepper

TO SERVE
thick ribbon pasta
circles of lemon rind, boiled to soften
** (optional)**

Lay the veal escalopes between 2 sheets of clingfilm or nonstick baking paper and beat as thinly as possible with a rolling pin or meat mallet. Mix the flour, paprika and salt and pepper to taste together on a plate, then lightly coat each escalope in the seasoned flour.

Heat 2 tablespoons of the oil in a large frying pan over a medium-high heat. Add the veal escalopes and cook for 1 minute on each side or until golden and crisp (you may have to use 2 pans or cook the veal in 2 batches). Remove with a slotted spoon and keep warm.

Reduce the heat to medium-low. Squeeze the juice of 1 lemon into the pan with the remaining oil and stir with a wooden spatula to scrape up any sediment from the pan. Cut the remaining lemon into slices and add to the pan with the olives. Leave to bubble for a few seconds, then remove from the heat and sprinkle over the chervil.

Put the escalopes on warmed serving plates and pour over the mixture in the pan. Serve immediately, with thick ribbon pasta and the circles of lemon rind, if using, garnished with chervil.

220 Lamb with salmoriglio sauce

Preparation time:
10 minutes

Cooking time:
15 minutes

Serves: **4**

8 loin lamb chops or 4 large chump chops
1 tablespoon chopped fresh oregano
2 tablespoons chopped flat leaf parsley
1 tablespoon capers, drained, rinsed and
** chopped**
1 teaspoon dried oregano
3 garlic cloves, crushed
finely grated rind and juice of 1 small
** lemon**
150 ml (¼ pint) extra virgin olive oil, plus
** extra for brushing**
salt and pepper

Trim any excess fat from the chops. If using loin chops, tie each chop into a neat shape with fine string.

Mix the fresh oregano, parsley and capers together on a chopping board, then transfer to a bowl with the dried oregano, garlic, lemon rind and juice, oil and salt and pepper to taste. Whisk well until combined.

Lightly brush a ridged griddle pan with oil and heat until smoking. Add the chops and cook for 6–7 minutes on each side, brushing halfway through with a little of the sauce. Alternatively, cook under a preheated high grill. Serve with the remaining sauce.

COOK'S NOTES With their lemony, garlicky, herby sauce, these lamb chops are ideal for alfresco dining and show how an unfussy meal can be really special. The salmoriglio sauce can be made several hours in advance for added convenience.

221 Steak with Roquefort sauce

222 Veal saltimbocca

Preparation time:
10 minutes

Cooking time:
4–5 minutes

Serves: **4**

25 g (1 oz) butter
4 fillet steaks, about 150 g (5 oz) each
cauliflower mash, to serve

SAUCE
1 garlic clove, crushed
25 g (1 oz) parsley leaves, roughly chopped
15 g (½ oz) mint leaves, roughly chopped
1 tablespoon roughly chopped walnuts
75 ml (3 fl oz) extra virgin olive oil
2 tablespoons walnut oil
50 g (2 oz) Roquefort cheese, crumbled
15 g (½ oz) Parmesan cheese, freshly grated
salt and pepper

To make the sauce, put the garlic, parsley, mint, walnuts and oils in a food processor and process until fairly smooth.

Add the Roquefort and Parmesan, process again and season to taste with salt and pepper.

Heat the butter in a heavy-based frying pan. Season the steaks to taste with salt and pepper, add to the pan and cook for 2 minutes each side for rare or a little longer for medium rare.

Transfer the steaks to warmed serving plates, top with the cheese sauce and serve immediately with cauliflower mash.

Preparation time:
10 minutes

Cooking time:
10–15 minutes

Serves: **4**

2 teaspoons plain flour
8 small veal escalopes
50 g (2 oz) butter
8 slices of prosciutto
8 large sage leaves
250 ml (8 fl oz) dry white wine
salt and pepper

Season the flour to taste with salt and pepper. Lay the veal escalopes between 2 layers of clingfilm or nonstick baking paper and beat as thinly as possible with a rolling pin or meat mallet. Lightly coat the escalopes in the seasoned flour.

Heat half the butter in a large, heavy-based frying pan over a medium-high heat. Add the escalopes, in batches, and cook for 1 minute on each side or until golden and crisp. Remove with a slotted spoon to a plate.

Lay a slice of prosciutto and 1 sage leaf on the centre of each escalope, return to the pan and cook for a further 2–3 minutes, carefully turning each escalope once to sear the prosciutto and sage. Remove with a slotted spoon to warmed serving plates.

Pour the wine into the pan and leave to bubble until reduced by about half. Cut the remaining butter into pieces and whisk into the wine. Season to taste with salt and pepper and pour the sauce over the escalopes to serve.

COOK'S NOTES Any remaining sauce can be stored, topped with a layer of oil, in a screw-top jar in the refrigerator for up to 5 days.

COOK'S NOTES Bashed thin, veal escalopes are quick to cook and stay moist and tender. The quantities can be easily halved if you are cooking for only two.

223 Pork patties with soured cream sauce

224 Fillet steak with horseradish cream

Preparation time:
20 minutes

Cooking time:
10 minutes

Serves: **4**

500 g (1 lb) lean minced pork
40 g (1½ oz) breadcrumbs
1 small onion, grated
1 teaspoon paprika
1 egg, beaten
**8 slices of pancetta or thin rashers of
   smoked streaky bacon**
25 g (1 oz) butter
1 tablespoon vegetable oil
150 ml (¼ pint) soured cream
2 tablespoons chopped dill
**2 teaspoons pink or green peppercorns,
   lightly crushed**
salt and pepper

Put the pork, breadcrumbs, onion, paprika, egg and a little seasoning in a bowl and mix until evenly combined. This is most easily done with your hands.

Divide the mixture into 8 equal pieces and pat them into burger shapes. Wrap a slice of pancetta or streaky bacon around each one, securing it with a wooden cocktail stick.

Melt the butter with the oil in a large, heavy-based frying pan and gently fry the patties for 5 minutes on each side until golden. Drain and transfer to serving plates. Add the soured cream, dill and peppercorns to the pan and heat gently, stirring, until smooth and creamy. Season to taste and serve with the patties.

Preparation time:
5 minutes

Cooking time:
2–12 minutes

Serves: **4**

1 teaspoon vegetable oil
4 fillet steaks, about 125 g (4 oz) each
shredded lettuce leaves, to serve

HORSERADISH CREAM
175 ml (6 fl oz) Greek yogurt
65 g (2½ oz) walnuts, chopped
40 g (1½ oz) horseradish sauce

To make the horseradish cream, mix all the ingredients together in a small bowl.

Heat a ridged griddle pan until smoking and brush the surface with the oil. Add the steaks and cook, turning once only to achieve a decorative ridged effect. The following timing is a rough guide for steaks that are about 2.5 cm (1 inch) thick – blue: 1–2 minutes on each side (soft with no feel of resistance); rare: 2–3 minutes on each side (soft and spongy; may still ooze some red meat juices when pressed); medium rare: 3–4 minutes on each side (a little firmer); medium: 4–5 minutes on each side (firm to the touch); well done: over 5 minutes on each side (solid).

Serve the steaks accompanied by the horseradish cream and shredded lettuce leaves.

COOK'S NOTES These little patties make a quick and easy supper dish and, once shaped, can be frozen if you don't want to cook them all. Serve with chunky chips and a herb salad.

9 Desserts

225 Summer fruit compote

226 Summer berry sorbet

Preparation time:
5 minutes, plus cooling

Cooking time:
5 minutes

Serves: **2**

250 g (8 oz) mixed summer berries, such as raspberries, blueberries and strawberries, defrosted if frozen
finely grated rind and juice of 1 large orange
1 tablespoon redcurrant jelly
250 ml (8 fl oz) natural yogurt, to serve

Put the berries, orange rind and juice and redcurrant jelly in a large, heavy-based saucepan. Cover and cook gently for 5 minutes or until the juices start to flow and the fruit is softened. Remove from the heat and leave to cool.

Divide the compote between 2 serving dishes and serve with the yogurt.

Preparation time:
5 minutes, plus freezing

Cooking time:
No cooking

Serves: **2**

250 g (8 oz) frozen mixed summer berries
75 ml (3 fl oz) spiced berry cordial
2 tablespoons Kirsch
1 tablespoon lime juice

Put all the ingredients in a blender or food processor and blend to a smooth purée. Be careful not to over-process as this will soften the mixture too much.

Spoon the sorbet into a chilled shallow plastic container and freeze for 25 minutes. Spoon into bowls and serve immediately.

COOK'S NOTES You can use any combination of berries for this compote and it would also make a lovely light breakfast. For an extra touch of sweetness, drizzle a little runny honey on top of the desserts.

227 Pink grapefruit parfait

228 Raspberry and shortcake mess

Preparation time:
15 minutes

Cooking time:
No cooking

Serves: **4**

2 pink grapefruits
5 tablespoons soft dark brown sugar,
   plus extra for sprinkling
250 ml (8 fl oz) double cream
150 ml (¼ pint) Greek yogurt
3 tablespoons elderflower cordial
½ teaspoon ground ginger
½ teaspoon ground cinnamon
brandy snaps, to serve (optional)

Preparation time:
5 minutes

Cooking time:
No cooking

Serves: **4**

300 g (10 oz) raspberries, defrosted if
   frozen, roughly crushed
4 shortbread fingers, roughly crushed
400 g (13 oz) fromage frais
2 tablespoons icing sugar

Finely grate the rind of one grapefruit, avoiding any of the bitter white pith. Remove the peel and pith from both grapefruits, then cut between the membranes to remove the segments. Put in a large dish, sprinkle with 2 tablespoons of the sugar and set aside.

Whisk the cream and yogurt together in a large bowl until thick but not stiff. Fold in the elderflower cordial, spices, grapefruit rind and remaining sugar until smooth. Pour the mixture into attractive glasses, arranging the grapefruit segments between layers of parfait. Sprinkle the top with extra sugar and serve immediately, accompanied with brandy snaps, if you like.

Reserving a few raspberries for decoration, gently combine all the remaining ingredients in a bowl.

Divide among 4 serving dishes. Decorate with the reserved raspberries and serve immediately.

COOK'S NOTES This recipe is perfect for a lazy summer lunch. It also works really well with orange segments and chocolate shavings in place of the grapefruit and ginger.

229 Chocolate and raspberry soufflés

Preparation time:
10 minutes

Cooking time:
12–15 minutes

Serves: **4**

Oven temperature:
190°C (375°F) Gas Mark 5

100 g (3½ oz) plain dark chocolate
3 eggs, separated
50 g (2 oz) self-raising flour, sifted
40 g (1½ oz) caster sugar
150 g (5 oz) raspberries, plus extra to
serve (optional)
unsalted butter, for greasing
sifted icing sugar, to decorate

Break the chocolate into squares and put in a heatproof bowl set over a saucepan of simmering water, then leave until melted.

Transfer the melted chocolate to a large bowl and whisk in the egg yolks. Fold in the flour.

Whisk the egg whites and caster sugar in a medium bowl until soft peaks form. Beat a spoonful of the egg whites into the chocolate mixture to loosen, then gently fold in the remainder.

Divide the raspberries among 4 lightly greased ovenproof ramekins, pour over the chocolate mixture, then bake in a preheated oven, 190°C (375°F), Gas Mark 5, for 12–15 minutes until the soufflés have risen.

Dust with sifted icing sugar to decorate and serve with extra raspberries, if you like.

COOK'S NOTES Many people shy away from soufflés as they think it's almost impossible to get them to rise perfectly. In fact, they're not really that difficult. The secret is to get them to the table as soon as possible, before they start to deflate.

230 Orange, rhubarb and ginger slump

Preparation time:
10 minutes

Cooking time:
about 20 minutes

Serves: **6**

Oven temperature:
200°C (400°F) Gas Mark 6

750 g (1½ lb) rhubarb, chopped into 1.5 cm
(¾ inch) pieces
½ teaspoon ground ginger
50 g (2 oz) golden caster sugar
finely grated rind and juice of 1 orange
4 tablespoons mascarpone cheese
175 g (6 oz) self-raising flour
50 g (2 oz) unsalted butter, diced
finely grated rind of ½ lemon
6 tablespoons milk
ready-made custard, to serve

Put the rhubarb, ginger, half the sugar and orange rind and juice in a medium saucepan. Bring to the boil, then reduce the heat and simmer gently for 5–6 minutes until the rhubarb is just tender. Transfer to an ovenproof dish and spoon over dollops of the mascarpone.

Sift the flour into a bowl. Add the butter and rub in with the fingertips until the mixture resembles fine breadcrumbs. Quickly stir in the remaining sugar, the lemon rind and milk until combined. Arrange spoonfuls of the mixture over the rhubarb and mascarpone.

Bake in a preheated oven, 200°C (400°F), Gas Mark 6, for 12–15 minutes until golden and bubbling. Serve with custard.

231 Vanilla and banana pancakes

232 Drunken orange slices

Preparation time:
15 minutes

Cooking time:
about 15 minutes

Serves: **4**

2 bananas
1 teaspoon vanilla extract
150 g (5 oz) self-raising flour
1 teaspoon baking powder
1 tablespoon caster sugar
1 egg
75 ml (3 fl oz) milk
1 tablespoon unsalted butter, melted
sunflower oil, for frying
maple syrup or maple syrup butter (see Cook's Notes), to serve

Preparation time:
15 minutes

Cooking time:
12 minutes

Serves: **4**

4 large sweet oranges
4 tablespoons cold water
4 tablespoons brown sugar
3 tablespoons Cointreau
2 tablespoons whisky
juice of 1 small orange
1 vanilla pod, split
1 cinnamon stick
4 cloves
2–3 mace blades (optional)
ginger or other ice cream, to serve

Mash the bananas with the vanilla extract in a bowl to make a smooth purée. Sift the flour and baking powder into a separate bowl and stir in the sugar.

Beat the egg, milk and melted butter together in another bowl and beat into the dry ingredients until smooth. Stir in the banana purée.

Heat a little oil in a large frying pan or griddle pan over a medium heat. Using a large metal spoon, drop 4 spoonfuls of the batter, well spaced apart, in the pan and cook for 2 minutes or until bubbles form on the surfaces and the undersides are golden brown. Using a spatula, turn the pancakes over and cook on the other side for 1–2 minutes. Remove from the pan, wrap in a tea towel and keep warm while cooking the remaining batter in the same way.

Transfer the pancakes to a serving plate and serve with maple syrup or maple syrup butter.

Using a small, sharp knife, cut off the base and the top of each orange. Cut down around the curve of the orange to remove all the peel and pith, leaving just the orange flesh. Cut the flesh horizontally into 5 mm (¼ inch) slices and set aside.

Put the measured water, sugar, 2 tablespoons of the Cointreau, the whisky, orange juice, vanilla pod, cinnamon stick, cloves and mace (if used) in a small saucepan and heat very gently until the sugar has dissolved. Increase the heat and boil vigorously for 5 minutes. Leave to cool slightly, but keep warm.

Heat a ridged griddle pan until smoking. Add the orange slices and cook for 1 minute on each side until caramelized. Sprinkle over the remaining Cointreau, flame with a match and stand well back. When the flames subside, transfer the orange slices to serving dishes and drizzle with the flamed syrup. Serve immediately with ginger ice cream or an ice cream of your choice.

COOK'S NOTES To make maple syrup butter, gradually beat 2 tablespoons maple syrup and 1 tablespoon icing sugar into 125 g (4 oz) softened unsalted butter, together with a few drops of vanilla extract, if you like. Cover and chill until required. It can be kept in the refrigerator for up to 1 week.

233 Peach strudel fingers

Preparation time:
15 minutes

Cooking time:
10–13 minutes

Serves: **4**

Oven temperature:
180°C (350°F) Gas Mark 4

3 ripe peaches, stoned and thinly sliced
2 tablespoons caster sugar, plus extra to decorate
2 tablespoons ground almonds
½ teaspoon ground cinnamon
2 tablespoons sultanas
6 sheets of filo pastry, each 30 x 18 cm (12 x 7 inches), defrosted if frozen
40 g (1½ oz) unsalted butter, melted
sifted icing sugar, to decorate
whipped cream or crème fraîche, to serve

Put the peaches in a bowl with the caster sugar, ground almonds, cinnamon and sultanas and toss gently together. Lay a sheet of filo pastry on a work surface, with the longest edge towards you, and brush with a little of the melted butter. Spoon a quarter of the peach mixture horizontally (or follow the longest edge) in a line down the centre, stopping about 5 cm (2 inches) from either end.

Fold the short sides of the pastry over the filling. Fold one long side over the filling, then roll up to enclose the filling completely. Transfer the strudel to a baking sheet. Repeat to make 3 more strudels.

Cut the remaining pastry sheets in half. Brush the outside edges of the strudels with a little more butter, then roll up in the remaining pastry sheets. Brush with the remaining butter.

Bake in a preheated oven, 180°C (350°F), Gas Mark 4, for 10–13 minutes until golden brown. Dust with a little sifted icing sugar and serve warm with whipped cream or crème fraîche.

COOK'S NOTES Filo pastry is perfect for making a simple, speedy strudel. You can also serve it with ice cream.

234 Apple fritters with blackberry sauce

Preparation time:
10 minutes

Cooking time:
about 15 minutes

Serves: **4**

2 eggs
125 g (4 oz) plain flour
4 tablespoons caster sugar
150 ml (¼ pint) milk
sunflower oil, for deep-frying
4 dessert apples, cored and thickly sliced
150 g (5 oz) frozen blackberries
2 tablespoons water
sifted icing sugar, to decorate

Separate one egg and put the white in one bowl and the yolk and the whole egg in a second bowl. Add the flour and half the caster sugar to the second bowl. Whisk the egg white until soft peaks form, then use the same whisk to beat the flour mixture until smooth, gradually whisking in the milk. Fold in the egg white.

Pour the oil into a saucepan until it comes one-third of the way up the side, then heat to 180–190°C (350–375°F) or until a cube of bread browns in 30 seconds. Add a few apple slices to the batter and turn gently to coat. Lift out one slice at a time with a fork and lower carefully into the oil. Cook, in batches, for 2–3 minutes, turning until evenly golden. Remove with a slotted spoon and drain on kitchen paper.

Meanwhile, put the blackberries, remaining sugar and measured water in a small saucepan and heat for 2–3 minutes until hot. Arrange the fritters on serving plates, spoon the blackberry sauce around and dust with a little sifted icing sugar.

COOK'S NOTES For an extra treat, serve with big scoops of vanilla ice cream. Thick slices of banana can be coated in this batter and cooked in the same way if you prefer.

235 Orange palmiers with plums

236 Barbecued fruits with palm sugar

Preparation time:
15 minutes
	1 sheet of ready-rolled frozen puff pastry,
	    about 25 cm (10 inches) square,
	    defrosted

Cooking time: **10 minutes**	**beaten egg, for brushing** **3 tablespoons light muscovado sugar** **finely grated rind of ½ orange**
Serves: **4**	**vegetable oil, for oiling** **6 tablespoons orange juice**
	50 g (2 oz) caster sugar
Oven temperature: **200°C (400°F) Gas Mark 6**	**400 g (13 oz) plums, stoned and sliced** **sifted icing sugar, to decorate** **crème fraîche, to serve**

Brush the pastry with some of the beaten egg, then sprinkle with the muscovado sugar and orange rind. Roll up one edge of the pastry until it reaches the centre. Repeat from the opposite edge until both rolls meet in the centre.

Brush with more beaten egg, then cut into 8 thick slices. Arrange on a lightly oiled baking sheet. Bake in a preheated oven, 200°C (400°F), Gas Mark 6, for 10 minutes until well risen and golden.

Meanwhile, put the orange juice and caster sugar into a saucepan. Add the plums and cook for 5 minutes.

Sandwich the palmiers in pairs with the plums, dust with sifted icing sugar and serve with crème fraîche.

COOK'S NOTES These crisp, delicate pastries look very professional, but they can be made in minutes, using ready-made and -rolled puff pastry. Vary the fruit for sandwiching between the pastries to suit the season – rhubarb, greengages and raspberries also work well.

Preparation time: **15 minutes**	**25 g (1 oz) palm sugar** **finely grated rind and juice of 1 lime** **2 tablespoons water**
Cooking time: **6–14 minutes**	**½ teaspoon cracked black peppercorns** **500 g (1 lb) mixed prepared fruit, such as** **pineapple slices, mango wedges and**
Serves: **4**	**peaches**
	TO SERVE **cinnamon or vanilla ice cream** **lime slices**

Put the sugar, lime rind and juice, measured water and peppercorns in a small saucepan and heat very gently until the sugar has dissolved. Remove from the heat and dip the base of the saucepan in ice-cold water to cool.

Brush the cooled syrup over the prepared fruits and cook over a preheated barbecue for 3–4 minutes on each side or under a preheated high grill for 6–7 minutes on each side until charred and tender.

Serve with scoops of cinnamon or vanilla ice cream and lime slices.

237 Almond angel cakes with berries

Preparation time:	sunflower oil, for oiling
15 minutes	4 egg whites
	3 tablespoons granulated sugar
Cooking time:	50 g (2 oz) ground almonds
10–12 minutes	generous pinch of cream of tartar
	15 g (½ oz) flaked almonds
Serves: 6	400 g (13 oz) frozen mixed berry fruits
	200 g (7 oz) fromage frais
Oven temperature:	1 tablespoon sifted icing sugar, to
180°C (350°F) Gas Mark 4	decorate (optional)

Lightly oil 6 sections of a deep muffin tin and line the bases with rounds of greaseproof paper.

Whisk the egg whites in a large bowl until stiff, moist peaks form. Whisk in the granulated sugar, a teaspoonful at a time, until it has all been added, then continue to whisk for 1–2 minutes until the mixture is thick and glossy.

Fold in the ground almonds and cream of tartar and spoon the mixture into the sections of the prepared muffin tin. Sprinkle the flaked almonds over the tops.

Bake in a preheated oven, 180°C (350°F), Gas Mark 4, for 10–12 minutes until golden brown and set. Loosen the edges of the cakes with a knife, then lift on to a cooling rack.

Warm the fruits in a saucepan. Arrange the angel cakes on serving plates, add a spoonful of fromage frais to each and spoon the fruits around. Dust with the icing sugar, if you like.

238 Roasted plums with ginger sauce

Preparation time:	625 g (1¼ lb) dessert plums
15 minutes	4 bay leaves
	100 ml (3½ fl oz) white wine
Cooking time:	2 tablespoons clear honey
10–15 minutes	50 g (2 oz) fresh root ginger, peeled
	1 tablespoon caster sugar
Serves: 6	75 ml (3 fl oz) water
	150 g (5 oz) white chocolate, chopped
Oven temperature:	100 g (3½ oz) crème fraîche
220°C (425°F) Gas Mark 7	

Halve and stone the plums, then arrange in a single layer in a roasting tin or shallow ovenproof dish in which they fit snugly. Tuck the bay leaves around them.

Mix together the wine and honey and pour over the plums. Roast in a preheated oven, 220°C (425°F), Gas Mark 7, for 10–15 minutes or until the plums begin to colour but still retain their shape.

Meanwhile, grate the ginger and put in a small, heavy-based saucepan, scraping the gratings from the board and grater into the pan. Add the sugar and measured water. Heat gently until the sugar has dissolved, then bring to the boil and boil for 1 minute. Strain into a clean pan. Add the chocolate and leave until melted, stirring frequently until smooth. If the chocolate doesn't melt, heat the mixture very gently. Stir in the crème fraîche.

To serve, warm the sauce through gently. Transfer the plums to serving dishes, spoon over the cooking juices and serve with the sauce.

COOK'S NOTES You can make this quick and easy pudding with almost any reasonably decent plums, because roasting in wine softens them and brings out their flavour.

239 Seared pineapple with plum sauce

240 Cranachan with raspberries

Preparation time:
20 minutes

Cooking time:
5–6 minutes

Serves: **6**

500 g (1 lb) ripe red plums, stoned and diced
6 star anise
generous pinch of chilli powder and ground cinnamon, or to taste
8 tablespoons water
1 large pineapple, about 800 g (1 lb 10 oz) prepared weight, cored and sliced
2 tablespoons sifted icing sugar
crème fraîche or ice cream, to serve (optional)

Put the plums, star anise, chilli powder, cinnamon and measured water in a saucepan, cover and simmer for 5 minutes until softened.

Meanwhile, halve the pineapple slices and arrange on a foil-lined grill rack. Dust with half the sugar and cook under a preheated grill for 2–3 minutes on each side until lightly browned.

Arrange the pineapple on serving plates, spoon the hot plum sauce by the side and dust with the remaining sugar. Serve immediately, with crème fraîche or ice cream, if you like.

Preparation time:
10 minutes, plus cooling

Cooking time:
5–8 minutes

Serves: **6**

Oven temperature:
180°C (350°F) Gas Mark 4

40 g (1½ oz) medium oatmeal
150 ml (¼ pint) whipping cream
200 g (7 oz) fromage frais
2 tablespoons thick-set honey, preferably lavender or other flower honey
250 g (8 oz) raspberries, just defrosted if frozen

Put the oatmeal in a shallow baking tin and toast in a preheated oven, 180°C (350°F), Gas Mark 4, stirring once, for 5–8 minutes until evenly browned. Leave to cool.

Whip the cream in a large bowl until it forms soft peaks. Fold in the fromage frais, then the honey and, finally, the cooled oatmeal.

Reserving a few raspberries to top the desserts, divide half the remaining raspberries among 6 small glass dishes. Spoon half the cream mixture on top, then repeat the layering with the other raspberries and the remaining cream mixture. Arrange the reserved raspberries on top and serve.

COOK'S NOTES Sweetened with natural sugars and just a light dusting of icing sugar, this fresh-tasting, eye-catching dessert can be quickly and simply put together when time is short. The riper the plums you use, the sweeter they will be. If you can find only under-ripe fruit, sweeten them with a little light cane sugar.

COOK'S NOTES The oatmeal can be toasted well in advance, but it is best to mix it with the cream only at the last minute because oatmeal swells with standing.

241 Baked pear with almond crumble

Preparation time:
10 minutes

Cooking time:
20 minutes

Serves: **4**

Oven temperature:
220°C (425°F) Gas Mark 7

75 g (3 oz) wholemeal flour
65 g (2½ oz) ground almonds
75 g (3 oz) soft light brown sugar
65 g (2½ oz) unsalted butter, diced
4 pears, quartered, cored and sliced
  lengthways
juice of 1 lime
2 tablespoons flaked almonds
150 g (5 oz) crème fraîche, to serve
  (optional)

Mix together the flour, ground almonds and sugar in a large bowl. Add the butter and rub in with the fingertips until the mixture resembles fine breadcrumbs.

Arrange the pear slices in 4 tall, ovenproof ramekins and drizzle with the lime juice. Cover the pears with the crumble mixture and sprinkle over the flaked almonds.

Bake in a preheated oven, 220°C (425°F), Gas Mark 7, for 20 minutes. Serve warm, topped with the crème fraîche, if you like.

242 Peach and raspberry tartlets

Preparation time:
15 minutes

Cooking time:
8–10 minutes

Serves: **4**

Oven temperature:
190°C (375°F) Gas Mark 5

15 g (½ oz) butter, melted
4 sheets of filo pastry, each about 25 cm
  (10 inches) square, defrosted if frozen
125 ml (4 fl oz) double cream
1 tablespoon soft light brown sugar
2 ripe peaches, skinned, halved, stoned
  and sliced
50 g (2 oz) raspberries
sifted icing sugar, to decorate

Grease 4 deep muffin tins with the melted butter. Cut a sheet of filo pastry in half, then across into 4 equal squares. Use the filo pastry squares to line one muffin tin, arranging them at slightly different angles. Press down well, tucking the pastry into the tin neatly. Repeat with the remaining pastry sheets.

Bake the tartlet cases in a preheated oven, 190°C (375°F), Gas Mark 5, for 8–10 minutes or until golden. Carefully remove the tartlet cases from the tins and leave to cool on a wire rack.

Meanwhile, pour the cream into a bowl and add the sugar. Whip lightly until it holds its shape. Spoon the cream into the tartlet cases and top with the peaches and raspberries. Dust with icing sugar and serve immediately.

COOK'S NOTES The tartlet cases can be baked several hours in advance for added flexibility, but should be filled just before eating to prevent the pastry from going soft.

243 Pears with minted mascarpone

244 Hot berries with orange cream

Preparation time:
10 minutes

Cooking time:
5 minutes

Serves: **4**

30 g (1¼ oz) unsalted butter
2 tablespoons clear honey
4 ripe dessert pears, such as Red William, cored and sliced lengthways
lemon juice, for sprinkling

MINTED MASCARPONE
1 tablespoon finely chopped mint
1 tablespoon granulated sugar
175 g (6 oz) mascarpone cheese

TO DECORATE
mint sprigs
sifted icing sugar
ground cinnamon

Melt the butter in a small saucepan. Remove from the heat and stir in the honey.

Sprinkle the pear slices with a little lemon juice as soon as they are prepared to prevent them from discolouring. Line a baking sheet with foil and lay the pear slices on it. Brush the pears with the butter and honey mixture. Cook the pears under a preheated grill on its highest setting for 5 minutes.

Meanwhile, to make the minted mascarpone, lightly whisk the mint and granulated sugar into the mascarpone in a bowl.

Divide the pear slices among 4 plates and add a dollop of the minted mascarpone. Decorate each portion with a mint sprig, then lightly dust with icing sugar and cinnamon and serve immediately.

COOK'S NOTES Mascarpone is a soft cheese that is used in many sweet and savoury Italian dishes. It takes well to other flavours, and the mint in this quick dessert gives it a lovely fresh flavour.

Preparation time:
15 minutes

Cooking time:
5–8 minutes

Serves: **4**

150 ml (¼ pint) Greek yogurt
125 ml (4 fl oz) single cream
1 egg yolk
1 teaspoon orange flower water
1 orange, peeled and pith removed, separated into segments
150 g (5 oz) blueberries
150 g (5 oz) strawberries, hulled and cut into bite-sized pieces

Mix together the yogurt, cream, egg yolk and orange flower water in a medium-sized bowl.

Mix together all the fruit in a separate bowl.

Divide the fruit among 4 ovenproof serving dishes, then spoon the yogurt mixture over to cover the fruit.

Cook under a preheated high grill for 5–8 minutes until the cream starts to bubble and turn brown. Serve immediately, being sure to warn your guests about the hot dishes.

245 Pears with chocolate crumble

Preparation time:
10 minutes

Cooking time:
8 minutes

Serves: **4**

50 g (2 oz) light muscovado sugar
150 ml (¼ pint) water
25 g (1 oz) raisins
½ teaspoon ground cinnamon
4 ripe dessert pears, peeled, halved and cored
40 g (1½ oz) unsalted butter
50 g (2 oz) porridge oats
25 g (1 oz) hazelnuts, roughly chopped
50 g (2 oz) plain dark or milk chocolate, chopped
lightly whipped cream or Greek yogurt, to serve (optional)

Put half the sugar in a frying pan or wide sauté pan with the measured water, raisins and cinnamon. Bring just to the boil and add the pears. Reduce the heat and simmer gently for 5 minutes or until the pears are slightly softened.

Meanwhile, melt the butter in a separate frying pan or saucepan. Add the porridge oats and cook gently for 2 minutes. Stir in the remaining sugar and cook over a low heat until golden.

Spoon the pears on to serving plates. Stir the hazelnuts and chocolate into the oat mixture. Once the chocolate starts to melt, spoon over the pears. Serve topped with whipped cream or Greek yogurt, if you like.

246 Waffles with berry compote

Preparation time:
10 minutes

Cooking time:
20 minutes

Serves: **2**

65 g (2½ oz) strawberries, hulled and quartered
65 g (2½ oz) raspberries
65 g (2½ oz) blueberries
1 tablespoon elderflower cordial
2 tablespoons Greek yogurt, to serve

WAFFLES
50 ml (2 fl oz) milk
1 egg, separated
40 g (1½ oz) unsalted butter, melted, plus extra for greasing
50 g (2 oz) self-raising wholemeal flour
1½ tablespoons icing sugar, sifted
finely grated rind of ¼ lemon

To make the waffles, pour the milk into a bowl, add the egg yolk and whisk lightly. Add 2 teaspoons of the melted butter and work in lightly with a fork.

Heat a waffle iron on the hob or preheat an electric one while you sift the flour into a bowl. Make a well in the centre of the flour and gradually beat in the milk mixture and the remaining melted butter. Whisk the egg white in a separate bowl until stiff, moist peaks form, then fold into the batter with 2 teaspoons of the icing sugar and the lemon rind. Grease the waffle iron and pour in about a quarter of the batter. Close and cook for 4–5 minutes, turning once or twice if using a hob-top model. When the waffle is golden brown, cover and keep warm while you cook the remainder.

Meanwhile, put all the berries and the elderflower cordial in a small saucepan and heat gently until the juices just start to flow.

Put 2 waffles on each plate and serve with the berries and a spoonful of Greek yogurt.

247 Strawberry and lavender crush

Preparation time:
10 minutes

Cooking time:
No cooking

Serves: **4**

400 g (13 oz) strawberries
2 tablespoons icing sugar, plus extra for decorating
4–5 lavender flowers, plus extra to decorate
400 ml (14 fl oz) Greek yogurt
4 ready-made meringue nests

Reserving 4 small strawberries for decoration, hull and mash the remainder with the icing sugar using a fork or a blender or food processor. Pick the individual lavender flowers from the stems and crumble into the strawberry mixture to taste.

Put the yogurt in a bowl, crumble in the meringues, then lightly mix together. Add the strawberry mixture, fold together with a spoon until marbled, then spoon into 4 glasses.

Cut the reserved strawberries in half, then decorate the desserts with the strawberry halves and extra lavender flowers. Lightly dust with icing sugar and serve immediately.

COOK'S NOTES Capture the essence of summer with this delicately flavoured, light strawberry and meringue dessert in a matter of moments. If you don't have fresh lavender at home, buy a small pot from a garden centre or use a few dried flowers instead.

248 Cherry and cinnamon zabaglione

Preparation time:
10 minutes

Cooking time:
about 10 minutes

Serves: **4**

4 egg yolks
125 g (4 oz) caster sugar
150 ml (¼ pint) cream sherry
large pinch of ground cinnamon
400 g (13 oz) can black cherries in syrup
2 amaretti biscuits, crumbled, to decorate

Pour 5 cm (2 inches) water into a medium saucepan and bring to the boil. Set a large heatproof bowl over the pan, making sure that the water does not touch the base of the bowl. Reduce the heat so that the water is simmering, then add the egg yolks, sugar, sherry and cinnamon to the bowl. Whisk for 5–8 minutes until very thick and foamy and the custard leaves a trail when the whisk is lifted above the mixture.

Drain off some of the cherry syrup and then tip the cherries and just a little of the syrup into a small saucepan. Warm through, then spoon into 4 glasses. Pour the warm zabaglione over the top and decorate with crumbled amaretti biscuits. Serve immediately.

COOK'S NOTES A classic Italian dessert, zabaglione makes the perfect partner for warmed cherries and a great standby for unexpected guests. Measure out the ingredients before you sit down to your main course so that you can whip up the dessert in a few minutes.

249 Soufflé berry omelette

250 Nectarine and blueberry tartlets

Preparation time:	6 eggs, separated
15 minutes	**2 teaspoons vanilla extract**
	4 tablespoons icing sugar
Cooking time:	**40 g (1½ oz) unsalted butter**
5–8 minutes	**4 tablespoons raspberry jam**
	100 g (3½ oz) raspberries, defrosted if
Serves: **4**	**frozen**
	100 g (3½ oz) blueberries, defrosted if
	frozen
	single cream, to serve

Whisk the egg whites in a large bowl until soft peaks form. Put the egg yolks, vanilla extract and 1 tablespoon of the sugar in a separate bowl and use the same whisk to beat together. Fold a spoonful of the egg whites into the yolk mixture to loosen, then add the remainder and fold in gently with a large metal spoon.

Heat half the butter in a 20 cm (8 inch) frying pan. Pour in half the egg mixture and cook for 3–4 minutes until the underside is golden. Quickly flash the omelette under a preheated high grill for 1–2 minutes to brown the top. Slide into a shallow dish and quickly make a second omelette in the same way with the remaining ingredients.

Dot the omelettes with the jam and berries, then fold in half to enclose the filling. Dust the tops with the remaining sugar, cut in half and serve immediately with cream.

Preparation time:	25 g (1 oz) butter
15 minutes	**2 teaspoons olive oil**
	4 sheets of filo pastry, each 30 x 18 cm
Cooking time:	**(12 x 7 inches) or 65 g (2½ oz) in total,**
6–8 minutes	**defrosted if frozen**
	2 tablespoons red berry jam
Makes: **12**	**juice of ½ orange**
	4 ripe nectarines, halved, stoned and
Oven temperature:	**sliced**
180°C 350°F Gas Mark 4	**150 g (5 oz) blueberries**
	sifted icing sugar, to decorate
	fromage frais or yogurt ice cream, to
	serve

Melt the butter with the oil in a small saucepan. Separate the filo pastry sheets and brush lightly with the butter mixture, then cut into 24 pieces, each about 10 x 8 cm (4 x 3 inches).

Arrange a piece of filo in each section of a deep 12-hole muffin tin, then add a second piece at a slight angle to the first to give a jagged edge to each pastry case.

Bake the tartlet cases in a preheated oven, 180°C (350°F), Gas Mark 4, for 6–8 minutes until golden. Meanwhile, warm the jam and orange juice in a saucepan, then add the nectarines and blueberries and warm through.

Carefully remove the tartlet cases from the tin and transfer to a serving dish. Fill with the warm fruit mixture and dust with sifted icing sugar to decorate. Serve with spoonfuls of fromage frais or yogurt ice cream.

COOK'S NOTES These light, fluffy soufflé omelettes can be made in just a few minutes. Frozen berries make a great standby and they can be quickly defrosted in the microwave if you haven't had an opportunity to buy fresh fruit.

251 Banana samosas with stem ginger cream

Preparation time:
20 minutes

Cooking time:
5–10 minutes

Serves: **4**

2 bananas
1 tablespoon soft brown sugar
12 filo pastry sheets, each about
  30 x 18 cm (12 x 7 inches)
oil for deep-frying

STEM GINGER CREAM
4 pieces of preserved stem ginger, finely
  diced
2 tablespoons syrup from the ginger
100 ml (3½ fl oz) double cream
icing sugar, to dust

Coarsely mash the bananas in a bowl and add the sugar. Mix well and set aside.

Fold a sheet of filo pastry in half lengthways. Place 2 tablespoons of the banana mixture at one end of the filo, then fold the corner of the pastry over the mixture, covering it in a triangle shape. Fold the triangle of pastry and filling over and over along the length of the filo to make a neat triangular samosa. Moisten the edge with water at the end to seal it in place. Repeat with the remaining filling and sheets of filo pastry.

Heat the oil for deep-frying to 180–190°C (350–375°F) or until a cube of bread browns in 30 seconds. Deep-fry the samosas in 2–3 batches, according to the size of pan, for 3–4 minutes until golden brown.

Use a slotted spoon to remove the samosas from the pan and place on kitchen paper to drain.

To make the stem ginger cream, mix the ginger with the syrup. Lightly whip the cream until it is just firm, then fold in the ginger and syrup.

Dust the samosas lightly with icing sugar and serve hot or warm with the ginger cream.

252 Banana and cardamom filo parcels

Preparation time:
15 minutes

Cooking time:
15 minutes

Serves: **4**

Oven temperature:
200°C (400°F) Gas Mark 6

3 large bananas
3 tablespoons demerara sugar
½ teaspoon ground cardamom
4 sheets of filo pastry, each 40 x 28 cm
  (16 x 11 inches), defrosted if frozen
15 g (1 oz) unsalted butter, melted, plus
  extra for greasing
1 tablespoon sesame seeds
Greek yogurt or fromage frais, to serve

Mash the bananas with the sugar and ground cardamom in a bowl to make a purée.

Lay a filo pastry sheet on a work surface, brush lightly with a little of the melted butter, then fold into thirds lengthways. Spoon a quarter of the banana mixture on to the pastry about 3.5 cm (1½ inches) from the end. Fold the left corner of the pastry diagonally to the right side of the pastry to cover the filling. Continue folding in the same way until you reach the end of the sheet. Repeat the process with the remaining pastry sheets to make 3 more parcels. Transfer the parcels to a lightly greased baking sheet, brush with the remaining melted butter and sprinkle over the sesame seeds.

Bake in a preheated oven, 200°C (400°F), Gas Mark 6, for 15 minutes or until golden. Serve hot with a spoonful of Greek yogurt or fromage frais.

COOK'S NOTES This is an unusual dessert that is easy to prepare but looks very impressive when served. The cardamom adds a warm spicy flavour to the sweet bananas.

253 Spice-infused fruit salad

254 Exotic fruit salad

Preparation time:
15 minutes

Cooking time:
5 minutes

Serves: **6**

1 vanilla pod
175 ml (6 fl oz) water
2½ tablespoons caster sugar
1 small hot red chilli, halved and
   deseeded
4 clementines
2 peaches
½ cantaloupe melon, deseeded
75 g (3 oz) blueberries

Use the tip of a small, sharp knife to score the vanilla pod lengthways through to the centre. Put the measured water and sugar in a medium pan and heat gently until the sugar has dissolved. Add the vanilla pod and chilli and heat gently for a further 2 minutes. Remove from the heat and leave to cool while you prepare the fruit.

Remove the peel from the clementines and slice the flesh. Stone and slice the peaches. Cut the melon flesh into small chunks, removing and discarding the skin.

Mix the fruit in a dish and pour over the warm syrup, discarding the chilli. Serve immediately or cover and chill until you are ready to serve.

Preparation time:
10 minutes, plus standing

Cooking time:
3 minutes

Serves: **1**

6 tablespoons apple juice
1 green cardamom pod, crushed
1 star anise
150 g (5 oz) pineapple, mango and
   kiwifruit
1 teaspoon toasted shredded coconut

Put the apple juice in a saucepan with the cardamom and star anise and bring to the boil. Remove from the heat and leave to stand for 10 minutes.

Meanwhile, peel, core and slice the pineapple, peel, stone and slice the mango and peel and slice the kiwifruit.

Put the prepared fruit in a bowl. Pour the juice mixture over the fruit and leave to stand for 5 minutes. Top with the coconut and serve.

COOK'S NOTES The 'hotness' of the syrup will depend on the type of chilli you use. Go for a small, fiery one, but remove it from the syrup before you pour it over the fruit so that it doesn't mask the warmth of the vanilla. Ideally, serve the fruit salad with scoops of vanilla ice cream for an icy-cool contrast.

255 Figs with yogurt and honey

256 Pancake stack with maple syrup

Preparation time:
5 minutes

Cooking time:
10 minutes

Serves: **4**

8 ripe figs
4 tablespoons natural yogurt
2 tablespoons clear honey

Preparation time:
10 minutes

Cooking time:
about 15 minutes

Serves: **4**

75 g (3 oz) unbleached plain flour
1 egg
125 ml (4 fl oz) milk
2½ tablespoons sunflower oil
1 tablespoon sugar
8 scoops of vanilla ice cream
maple syrup, to serve

Heat a griddle pan over a medium heat. Add the figs and cook for 8 minutes, turning occasionally, until charred on the outside. Remove and cut in half.

Arrange the figs on 4 plates and serve with a spoonful of yogurt and some honey drizzled over the top.

Put the flour, egg, milk, oil and sugar in a food processor and process until smooth and creamy.

Heat a large frying pan or ridged griddle pan over a medium heat. Using a large metal spoon, drop 4 tablespoonfuls of the batter, well spaced apart, in the pan and cook for 2 minutes or until bubbles form on the surfaces and the undersides are golden brown. Using a spatula, turn the pancakes over and cook on the other side for 1–2 minutes. Remove from the pan, wrap in a tea towel and keep warm while cooking the remaining batter in the same way, making 12 small pancakes in all.

Bring to the table as a stack, drizzled with maple syrup. Serve 3 pancakes to each person, with 2 scoops of ice cream.

COOK'S NOTES Buy figs when they are in season and full of flavour and juice to make this amazingly easy yet delicious dessert.

257 Chocolate risotto

Preparation time:	600 ml (1 pint) milk
5 minutes	**25 g (1 oz) granulated sugar**
	50 g (2 oz) butter
Cooking time:	**125 g (4 oz) risotto rice**
20 minutes	**50 g (2 oz) hazelnuts, toasted and chopped**
Serves: **4**	**50 g (2 oz) sultanas**
	125 g (4 oz) plain dark chocolate, grated, plus extra to decorate

Put the milk and sugar in a saucepan and bring to a gentle simmer.

Melt the butter in a separate, heavy-based saucepan. Add the rice and cook, stirring, for 1 minute. Add enough hot milk to just cover the rice and stir well. Simmer gently, stirring frequently.

When most of the liquid has been absorbed, add more milk. Continue adding the milk in stages and stirring until it has all been absorbed. Add the hazelnuts, sultanas and grated chocolate and mix quickly. Try not to overmix the chocolate, as the marbled effect looks attractive. Serve the risotto immediately, decorated with a little grated chocolate.

COOK'S NOTE For a special treat, add a splash of brandy just before decorating and serving the risotto.

258 Bananas with toffee sauce

Preparation time:	4 bananas
5 minutes	**125 g (4 oz) unsalted butter**
	125 g (4 oz) palm sugar
Cooking time:	**125 ml (4 fl oz) double cream**
5 minutes	**dash of lime juice, to taste**
	vanilla ice cream, to serve
Serves: **4**	**ground cinnamon or freshly grated nutmeg, to decorate (optional)**

Peel the bananas and cut them into quarters or in half lengthways. Melt the butter in a frying pan, add the bananas and cook for 30 seconds on each side or until lightly golden. Transfer to a warmed dish with a slotted spoon.

Stir the sugar and cream into the pan and heat gently until the sugar has dissolved. Simmer gently for 2–3 minutes until thickened. Add lime juice to taste.

Serve the bananas drizzled with the sauce and with a scoop of vanilla ice cream. Sprinkle with cinnamon or nutmeg to decorate, if you like.

259 Chocolate lime creams

260 Strawberries with chocolate spread

Preparation time:	100 g (3½ oz) plain dark chocolate
5 minutes, plus chilling	**50 g (2 oz) caster sugar**
	finely grated rind and juice of 2 limes
Cooking time:	**2 tablespoons water**
5 minutes	**300 ml (½ pint) double cream**

Serves: **4**

Preparation time:	200 g (7 oz) strawberries
5 minutes	**2 tablespoons chocolate hazelnut spread**
Cooking time:	
No cooking	

Serves: **1**

Coarsely grate the chocolate. Heat the sugar in a small, heavy-based saucepan with the lime rind and juice and water until the sugar has dissolved. Leave to cool slightly.

Put the lime syrup into a bowl with the cream and whisk until soft peaks form. Reserve a little of the grated chocolate. Fold the remainder into the cream mixture and spoon the mixture into serving glasses. Cover and chill in the freezer for 15 minutes, then serve sprinkled with the reserved grated chocolate.

Hull, then quarter or halve the strawberries.

Serve with the chocolate hazelnut spread for dipping.

COOK'S NOTES You can use milk chocolate instead of plain dark chocolate. Always buy good-quality chocolate with a high proportion of cocoa solids.

Index

Acknowledgements

Executive Editor Nicky Hill
Senior Editor Jessica Cowie
Executive Art Editor Penny Stock
Designer Ginny Zeal
Senior Production Controller Martin Croshaw
Picture Researcher Taura Riley

PICTURE ACKNOWLEDGEMENTS
Octopus Publishing Group Limited 90 right, 102 left, 117 right; /**Clive Bozzard-Hill** 85 left; /**Stephen Conroy** 17 left, 28 right, 37 left, 39 left, 39 right, 57 right, 59 right, 85 right, 87 left, 101 left, 114 left, 114 right, 115 left, 115 right, 133 right, 134 left, 134 right, 135 left, 144 left, 144 right, 145 left, 145 right, 146 right, 147 left; /**Gus Filgate** 25 left, 133 left; /**Sandra Lane** 32 left; /**William Lingwood** 10 left, 10 right, 12 left, 18 left, 18 right, 19 left, 22 left, 23 right, 24 left, 24 right, 29 right, 32 right, 44 right, 45 left, 45 right, 47 left, 49 left, 50 right, 54 left, 56 right, 62 right, 63 left, 64 left, 64 right, 65 left, 65 right, 66 left, 66 right, 67 left, 72 left, 74 left, 74 right, 75 left, 75 right, 77 left, 82 left, 89 left, 89 Right, 96 left, 96 right, 97 left, 97 right, 98 left, 98 right, 99 left, 99 right, 100 right, 106 left, 106 right, 107 left, 107 right, 108 left, 113 left, 116 left, 116 right, 117 right, 118 right, 119 left, 120 right, 121 left, 121 right, 127 right, 130 right, 131 left, 131 right, 132 left, 138 left, 142 left, 142 right, 143 left, 148 right, 149 left, 149 right, 150 left, 150 right, 151 right; /**David Loftus** 14 right, 15 right, 36 right, 38 right, 52 right, 53 left, 57 left, 59 left, 63 right, 69 right, 71 left, 71 right, 72 right, 73 left, 88 left, 88 right, 129 left, 154 left; /**Neil Mersh** 23 left, 84 right, 118 left, 151 left; /**Diana Miller** 16 left; /**Sean Myers** 105 right; /**Lis Parsons** 16 right, 28 left, 30 left, 30 right, 33 left, 34 right, 35 right, 36 left, 37 right, 42 left, 42 right, 43, 44 left, 46 left,49 right, 51 left, 51 right, 56 left, 58 left, 70 left, 70 right, 73 right, 77 right, 80 left, 81 left, 81 right, 82 right, 83 right, 86 left, 86 right, 100 left, 108 right, 109 right, 124 left, 125 left, 126 left, 126 right, 127 left, 128 right, 130 left, 135 right, 136 top left, 139 left, 139 right, 140 left, 140 right, 146 left, 147 right; /**William Reavell** 13 right, 15 left, 17 right, 19 left, 29 right, 34 right, 47 right, 48 right, 50 left, 52 right, 55 right, 62 left, 67 right, 68 right, 76 left, 76 right, 80 right, 90 left, 91 right, 92 left, 92 right, 93 left, 148 left; /**Gareth Sambidge** 13 left, 14 left, 22 right, 31 left, 35 left, 38 left, 43 right, 46 right, 48 left, 54 right, 69 left, 84 left, 87 right, 91 left, 93 right, 101 right, 102 right, 103 left, 103 right, 104 left, 104 right, 105 left, 109 left, 112 left, 112 right, 113 right, 119 right, 124 right, 125 right, 129 right, 132 right, 136 top right, 141 left, 141 right, 152 left, 152 right, 153 left, 153 right, 155 right; /**Simon Smith** 11 right; /**Ian Wallace** 12 right, 25 right, 31 right, 33 right, 55 left, 68 left, 83 left, 120 left, 128 left, 136 bottom right, 136 bottom left, 138 right, 143 right, 154 right, 259 left; /**Philip Webb** 11 left.